Neil Patrick Harris

Other books in the People in the News series:

Maya Angelou

Tyra Banks

Glenn Beck

David Beckham

Beyoncé

Sandra Bullock

Fidel Castro

Kelly Clarkson

Hillary Clinton

Miley Cyrus

Ellen Degeneres

Johnny Depp

Leonardo DiCaprio

Hilary Duff

Zac Efron

Brett Favre

50 Cent

Jeff Gordon

Al Gore

Tony Hawk

Salma Hayek

Jennifer Hudson

LeBron James

Jay-Z

Derek Jeter

Steve Jobs

Dwayne Johnson

Angelina Jolie

Jonas Brothers

Kim Jong II

Coretta Scott King

Ashton Kutcher

Spike Lee

George Lopez

Tobey Maguire

Eli Manning

John McCain

Barack Obama

Michelle Obama

Apolo Anton Ohno

Danica Patrick

Nancy Pelosi

Katy Perry

Tyler Perry

Queen Latifah

Daniel Radcliffe

Condoleezza Rice

Rihanna

Alex Rodriguez

Derrick Rose

J.K. Rowling

Shakira

Tupac Shakur

Will Smith

Gwen Stefani

Ben Stiller

Hilary Swank

Justin Timberlake

Usher

Denzel Washington

Serena Williams

Oprah Winfrey

people in the NEWS

Neil Patrick Harris

by Cherese Cartlidge

LUCENT BOOKS
A part of Gale, Cengage Learning

GALE
CENGAGE Learning·

Detroit • New York • San Francisco • New Haven, Conn • Waterville, Maine • London

LIBRARY OF CONGRESS CATALOGING-IN-PUBLICATION DATA

Cartlidge, Cherese.
  Neil Patrick Harris / by Cherese Cartlidge.
    p. cm. -- (People in the news)
  Includes bibliographical references and index.
  ISBN 978-1-4205-0615-0 (hardcover)
1. Harris, Neil Patrick, 1973---Juvenile literature. 2. Actors--United States--Biography--
Juvenile literature. I. Title.
  PN2287.H2493C38 2012
  792.02'8092--dc23
  [B]
                                                                        2011033382

Lucent Books
27500 Drake Rd
Farmington Hills MI 48331

ISBN-13: 978-1-4205-0615-0
ISBN-10: 1-4205-0615-3

Printed in the United States of America
1 2 3 4 5 6 7 15 14 13 12 11

Contents

Fame and celebrity are alluring. People are drawn to those who walk in fame's spotlight, whether they are known for great accomplishments or for notorious deeds. The lives of the famous pique public interest and attract attention, perhaps because their experiences seem in some ways so different from, yet in other ways so similar to, our own.

Newspapers, magazines, and television regularly capitalize on this fascination with celebrity by running profiles of famous people. For example, television programs such as *Entertainment Tonight* devote all their programming to stories about entertainment and entertainers. Magazines such as *People* fill their pages with stories of the private lives of famous people. Even newspapers, newsmagazines, and television news frequently delve into the lives of well-known personalities. Despite the number of articles and programs, few provide more than a superficial glimpse at their subjects.

Lucent's People in the News series offers young readers a deeper look into the lives of today's newsmakers, the influences that have shaped them, and the impact they have had in their fields of endeavor and on other people's lives. The subjects of the series hail from many disciplines and walks of life. They include authors, musicians, athletes, political leaders, entertainers, entrepreneurs, and others who have made a mark on modern life and who, in many cases, will continue to do so for years to come.

These biographies are more than factual chronicles. Each book emphasizes the contributions, accomplishments, or deeds that have brought fame or notoriety to the individual and shows how that person has influenced modern life. Authors portray their subjects in a realistic, unsentimental light. For example, Bill Gates—the cofounder of the software giant Microsoft—has been instrumental in making personal computers the most vital tool of the modern age. Few dispute his business savvy, his perseverance, or his technical expertise, yet critics say he is ruthless in his dealings with competitors and driven more by his desire to maintain Microsoft's dominance in the computer industry than by an interest in furthering technology.

In these books, young readers will encounter inspiring stories about real people who achieved success despite enormous obstacles. Oprah Winfrey—one of the most powerful, most watched, and wealthiest women in television history—spent the first six years of her life in the care of her grandparents while her unwed mother sought work and a better life elsewhere. Her adolescence was colored by pregnancy at age fourteen, rape, and sexual abuse.

Each author documents and supports his or her work with an array of primary and secondary source quotations taken from diaries, letters, speeches, and interviews. All quotes are footnoted to show readers exactly how and where biographers derive their information and provide guidance for further research. The quotations enliven the text by giving readers eyewitness views of the life and accomplishments of each person covered in the People in the News series.

In addition, each book in the series includes photographs, annotated bibliographies, timelines, and comprehensive indexes. For both the casual reader and the student researcher, the People in the News series offers insight into the lives of today's newsmakers—people who shape the way we live, work, and play in the modern age.

A Renaissance Man

Many of today's stars are fairly one-dimensional, meaning that their only talent is acting. Former teen idol Neil Patrick Harris, however, can be described as something of a Renaissance man—someone who is intelligent and accomplished in a variety of areas, and can act, sing, dance, play music, and perform live. He is just as versatile in his personal life; Harris is a socially adept and very likeable human being with a wide range of interests and friends, and his warm personality is evident both on and off the screen.

One person who has taken note of Harris's range of interests and talents is Debbie Reynolds, who played the part of Harris's grandmother in the CBS TV movie titled *The Christmas Wish* (1998). Reynolds is a screen legend who rose to fame as an actress, singer, and dancer in several musicals beginning in the 1950s, most notably in the classic 1952 comedy musical *Singin' in the Rain*. Upon learning he would get to work with Reynolds, Harris immediately went out and rented as many of her old movies as he could find. Reynolds recalls he would beg her every day on the set of *The Christmas Wish* to sing "Singin' in the Rain" for him, and soon he began singing it along with her. "He loves to sing," Reynolds said, adding that she found Harris "charming and sweet."[1]

As Reynolds learned, there is more to Neil Patrick Harris than a hardworking and multifaceted actor. Many people are surprised to learn that he is also an amateur magician and expert juggler.

8

He also writes, regularly posting comments on his Twitter page about his personal and professional life as well as his views on current events, and he has amassed an enormous following. There is also a tender side to Harris: He and his long-term partner recently adopted twins and have thrown themselves wholeheartedly into parenthood, an undertaking in which Harris gets to demonstrate his warmth and compassion on a daily basis.

"A Hollywood First"

Harris's career has spanned more than twenty years. He has gone from playing the baby-faced do-gooder Doogie Howser in the late 1980s and early 1990s to playing the phenomenal cad Barney Stinson today. He has found enormous popularity in both of these roles, which present characters who are unique and memorable in ways that are vastly different from each other. Both also have unique names; it seems that commonplace names just will not do for his most two popular

Harris has made a successful transition from child star to a popular and versatile adult actor.

characters, as Harris himself jokes in the book *It All Changed in an Instant: More Six-Word Memoirs by Writers Famous & Obscure*: "Barney . . . Doogie . . ! Average names elude me."[2]

It is only fitting that he play these two unique characters, for Harris himself is no average guy. His many talents as an entertainer and his warm, well-rounded personality have helped him successfully make the transition from child actor to adult actor and to find success in his professional life as well as happiness in his personal life. He is widely admired not just for his many talents, but also for his openness and honesty about his own life and his willingness to be open about his homosexuality. Above all, his ability to integrate his identity into his many talents, projects, and skills has made him one of Hollywood's most versatile stars. As a reporter for *New York* magazine put it, Harris is a "Hollywood first: an out gay actor who can host award shows, play a womanizer, walk the red carpet with his boyfriend, and then get cast in movies as a straight dad."[3]

An Entertainer for the New Millennium

Harris has also garnered much critical acclaim in recent years. In 2008 he was named to *Entertainment Weekly*'s Entertainers of the Year, an annual listing of the popular media magazine's picks for the top twenty-five entertainers. In 2011 he received another high honor when he was awarded a star on the Hollywood Walk of Fame. These two events demonstrate how Harris has grown beyond the confines of his childhood stardom to become one of today's hottest and most unique entertainers.

Harris is happy and well-adjusted, self-confident, and comfortable with who he is. His willingness to be openly gay has made him a role model to others who have struggled with their own sexual identity. This combination of his multifaceted talents and his easygoing acceptance of himself and others makes him not only a renaissance man, but a model of humanity for the twenty-first century.

Chapter 1

A Young Actor

Neil Patrick Harris was born on June 15, 1973, in Albuquerque, New Mexico. He is of Scottish, Irish, and English descent. His father, Ron Harris, and his mother, Sheila Scott Harris, were both lawyers. He has one older brother, Brian, who was born in 1970.

Growing Up in the Land of Enchantment

When Neil was still very young, the Harris family moved to Ruidoso, New Mexico, a small town about 120 miles (193km) south of Albuquerque. Known primarily as a mountain resort town that boasts skiing and the nearby Ruidoso Downs Race Track and Billy the Kid Casino, it was a tiny town compared with the city of Albuquerque. But it was also a quiet, safe community for the Harrises to raise their two sons. Adjacent to the Lincoln National Forest, Ruidoso is also a scenic place to grow up. Neil and his family spent plenty of time hiking, picnicking, and exploring the outdoors in New Mexico, nicknamed the Land of Enchantment.

One of Neil's favorite places to visit as a child was Carlsbad Caverns National Park, about 100 miles (161km) southeast of Ruidoso. Located within the park is an extensive limestone cavern that reaches a depth of 750 feet (229m). Tourists regularly hike or take an elevator down to see the many chambers, including one known as the Big Room, which is the third-largest limestone in the United States. To Neil, this underground system of caves was truly an enchanted place. "It's one of the most astonishing things I've ever seen. You just head down this gaping hole of darkness and it gets really chilly. And then you're just in this whole world like *The Lord of the Rings*. There's stalactites, stalagmites, there's individual paths you can take, there's audio things you can listen to," he recalled as an adult. "It's a pretty remarkable thing."[4]

Center of Attention

As a child, Neil showed an early interest in entertaining others. He started singing at home at a very young age, to the accompaniment of his father on a folk guitar. He loved to sing every chance he got, and the rosy-cheeked, curly-headed tot adored the attention he received. Soon he joined the choir at the Episcopal Church, where he could practice his singing on a regular basis.

He also became interested in magic and loved doing magic and card tricks. Neil enjoyed watching magicians perform on TV or in

Harris appears with his father, Ron, and mother, Sheila, at the opening night of Assassins in 2004. Harris's parents encouraged his love of performing from an early age.

Penn & Teller

Two of Neil Patrick Harris's childhood idols were magicians Penn Jillette and Raymond Teller, known collectively as Penn & Teller. Jillette is a raconteur (he gives improvised narratives by using images, sounds, and words) and Teller most often uses mime in performances. The two met in 1975 and began performing together, along with Weir Chrisimer, as the Asparagus Valley Cultural Society. By 1985 Penn & Teller had won an Emmy Award for their PBS special *Penn & Teller Go Public.* They toured nationally during the 1990s and appeared more than twenty times on *Late Night with David Letterman.* They have also appeared on several television shows, including *Miami Vice, Friends, Hollywood Squares,* and (as cartoons, voiced by Penn) *The Simpsons.*

Magicians Penn Jillette, left, and Raymond Teller were among Harris's childhood idols.

Penn & Teller are also the authors of three best-selling books: *Cruel Tricks for Dear Friends, How to Play with Your Food,* and *How to Play in Traffic.* They have also written articles for the *New York Times.* From 2003 to 2010 they appeared in a Showtime series that received eleven Emmy nominations and won the Writers Guild of America Award for Outstanding Comedy/Variety Series in 2004.

person and trying to figure out how they accomplished their tricks. Two of his favorites were Penn Jillette and Raymond Teller, better known as Penn & Teller. The two made several TV appearances, including the 1985 PBS special *Penn & Teller Go Public*. "They're the greatest!" Neil gushed as a teenager. "They're my idols!"[5]

Neil liked magic so much that whenever the family went to visit his grandparents in Albuquerque, he would spend his saved-up allowance money on magic props such as sponge balls and thumb tips. Then he would practice using these items over and over in the backseat of the car during the three-hour drive back to Ruidoso. Once he got the hang of a trick, he loved performing and catching others off guard with his magic. "He always wanted to make people laugh,"[6] recalls Ron Harris of his son's magic shows. Neil's enthusiasm for his hobby was apparent any time the Harris family had company. Whenever his mother would tell him it was time for him to stop performing for them, he would beg her, "Oh, come on, one more card trick."[7]

Playing Toto

When Neil was six years old, he discovered another love, some-what by accident. One day Brian, who was in the fourth grade, tried out for a part as a Munchkin in a school production of *The Wizard of Oz*. Neil decided to tag along with his big brother to the audition. When the director saw Neil, he decided the young boy was just right for the part of Toto, Dorothy's little dog. Neil explains that the primary reason he won the role was "because they needed someone small,"[8] and at age six, he fit the bill.

Playing Toto was just the beginning for Neil, who became interested in and serious about acting at a very early age. He absolutely loved the theater and began appearing in school plays every chance he got. He also loved to watch live performances and attend shows. This gave him another reason to look forward to visits with his grandparents, because he got to attend plays in Albuquerque. His first taste of professional live theater was the musical *Annie*. He went to Albuquerque with his family to see the Tony Award–winning musical. He recalls that when he was a child growing up in Ruidoso, "coming to Albuquerque and seeing a show was like Broadway, that was a big deal."[9]

Drama Camp Discovery

By the time Neil was fourteen years old, he had already appeared in numerous school and community productions. He had also made up his mind that he wanted to be an actor. Although both his parents were lawyers, and his older brother went to law school, Neil himself never considered a career as a lawyer. The only career path he was interested in was acting.

Mark Medoff

Mark Medoff is a playwright, screenwriter, actor, film and theatre director, and professor. He was born on March 6, 1940, in Mount Carmel, Illinois. He received a bachelor of arts degree from the University of Miami and a master's degree from Stanford University. In 1981 he was awarded an honorary degree from Gallaudet University.

Medoff is best known for writing the play *Children of a Lesser God*, for which he won a Tony Award and a Lawrence Olivier Award. He was also nominated for an Oscar for best screenplay for the movie adaptation of *Children of a Lesser God* (1986). In 1984 Medoff and Bruce Street cofounded the American Southwest Theatre Company, which is New Mexico State University's theater department. He has taught in the theatre arts department at New Mexico State University for more than twenty-seven years.

In 1988 Medoff discovered Neil Patrick Harris at the university's drama camp and cast him in the film *Clara's Heart*, for which Medoff wrote the screenplay. Medoff has also taught in the theatre departments briefly at Florida State University and the University of Houston. Medoff has three daughters with Stephanie Thorne, whom he married in 1972.

Neil's skill, natural talent, and onstage charisma led his drama teachers in Ruidoso to encourage him to attend a summer drama camp at New Mexico State University (NMSU) in Las Cruces. The camp, which was designed for children and teens, included a week of acting classes and writing instruction. "It was awesome," Harris recalls of the camp. "I'd never done anything like that before."[10]

Although Neil did not know it when he signed up for the camp, one of the professors in the theater department at NMSU was award-winning playwright Mark Medoff, who also served as director of the drama camp. When he met Neil, he was immediately impressed by the young boy's abilities as a performer. Medoff had just sold a script for a film titled *Clara's Heart*, which was based on the novel of the same name written by Joseph Olshan. Comedian and Academy Award–nominated actress Whoopi Goldberg had already been cast in the film as Clara, the tenderhearted nanny. But producers were still searching for someone to play the part of David, a wealthy, spoiled boy who is having difficulty dealing with his parents' divorce but eventually forms a deep bond with Clara.

Medoff thought Neil would be perfect for the part of David, so he asked him to make an audition tape. This was a huge break for the young boy from a small resort town in New Mexico. Although he had some experience onstage in minor productions, he had never done anything like acting in front of cameras or auditioning for a movie part. He was nervous when he made the tape, but it clearly displayed his talent. Hundreds of young boys tried out for the part. When Whoopi Goldberg saw Neil's audition tape, she asked to meet him. Neil flew with his family to California, where he visited Goldberg's beach house in Malibu. He was so starstruck he could barely speak to her.

Neil Patrick . . . Rocket?

Despite Neil's inexperience as an actor, he was eventually cast as David in *Clara's Heart*. At fourteen years old, he was ready to set out on his professional acting career. He even had an agent, Bo Shoots, who had tracked him down in Ruidoso and offered to represent him. Neil still faced one problem, however: his name.

Harris began his professional acting career with a role opposite Whoopi Goldberg in the 1988 film **Clara's Heart.**

There was already an actor named Neil Harris. The Screen Actors Guild, a labor union that represents more than two hundred thousand performers worldwide, has a rule that no two members of the union can use the exact same stage name. At first, Neil suggested stage names for himself such as Neil Danger Harris and Neil Patrick Rocket. Eventually, he, his parents, and his agent agreed that he would use all three of his given names as his stage name.

Working on the movie set was a dream come true for the young Neil Patrick Harris, though he often found himself intimidated by his costars. In addition to Goldberg, the cast included actors Michael Ontkean and Kathleen Quinlan, who played his parents. *Clara's Heart* was directed by award-winning TV and movie director Robert Mulligan, who was responsible for many notable films, including the 1962 classic *To Kill a Mockingbird*. Even after Neil got over being starstruck by his colleagues, making a movie still proved to be a big adjustment for him. During the filming, he traveled with the cast and crew to Maryland, New York, and

Jamaica, places he had never been. In addition, because it was his first film, he knew very little about the technical aspects of filmmaking and was sometimes confused about what he was supposed to do or where he was supposed to stand. But Goldberg, the director, and the rest of the cast took their young costar under their wings and guided him through the process. Exclaimed Neil in a later interview, "Whoopi is the absolute best!"[11]

Clara's Heart was only a moderate success at the box office and with critics. A reviewer for *Variety* had high praise for Neil's performance, though, saying the movie contained "a smashing screen debut for young Neil Patrick Harris."[12] For his role in the movie, Neil was nominated for a Golden Globe Award for Best Supporting Actor. He was thrilled to see his name alongside those of fellow nominees Alec Guinness, Raul Julia, Lou Diamond Phillips, and River Phoenix, as well as the award's winner, Martin Landau. Neil was also thrilled to have his work in *Clara's Heart* recognized with a Young Artist Award nomination for Best Young Actor in a Motion Picture (though he lost to Christian Bale for *Empire of the Sun*).

Sharing Screen Time with an Alien

By the time *Clara's Heart* was released in theaters in 1988, the Harris family had moved back to Albuquerque. There, his parents ran a restaurant named Perennials in the northeastern part of the city, while Neil attended public school at La Cueva High School. (Fellow actors Freddie Prinze Jr. and Christina July Kim are also among the school's alumni.) Neil continued acting every chance he got, and he also sang in the school choir. He also learned to pick his way through a song on the bass clarinet, French horn, oboe, tuba, and xylophone. While he was in high school, he appeared in many school plays and as a senior had a part in the school's production of *Fiddler on the Roof*. He also appeared in community theater, including a production of *Peter Pan* at Albuquerque's Musical Theatre Southwest.

Because of the recognition and respect he earned from his performance in *Clara's Heart*, Neil soon had more offers for

The teenaged Harris continued to pursue his acting career with stage and movie roles while attending high school.

professional acting jobs. In 1988 he appeared in his second motion picture, the children's classic movie *Purple People Eater*. This movie is based on the 1958 novelty song of the same name performed by character actor and singer Sheb Wooley. In the movie, Neil's character (Billy Johnson) plays the song, which prompts the appearance of a one-eyed purple alien that helps Billy come to the assistance of an elderly couple who have been evicted by their greedy landlord. Neil costarred with Ned Beatty, Shelley Winters, and Thora Birch. Also appearing in the movie were rock-and-roll legends Chubby Checker (as himself) and Little Richard (as the mayor).

Keeping Busy on TV

In the late 1980s Neil also appeared in several made-for-TV movies, which gave him further experience and exposure. The first of these was the NBC TV movie *Too Good to Be True* (1988). The plot of the movie involves a man who falls in love with a shady woman. Neil costarred in this movie with a large cast that included Loni Anderson, Patrick Duffy, Daniel Baldwin, and James B. Sikking. Most reviewers thought this movie did not live up to the quality of the 1945 classic film *Leave Her to Heaven*, on which it was based.

Next came *Cold Sassy Tree* (1989), based on the novel of the same name by Olive Ann Burns. In this Turner Network Television movie set at the turn of the twentieth century, Neil costarred with veteran actors Faye Dunaway and Richard Widmark. He played Will Tweedy, a boy who watches his newly widowed grandfather fall in love with an independent younger woman. Neil found himself

Harris appeared with veteran actor Richard Widmark, left, in the Turner Network Television movie Cold Sassy Tree *in 1989.*

once again working with big-name movie stars in *Cold Sassy Tree* and was at first somewhat intimidated by the Academy Award–winning Dunaway and the Golden Globe–winning Widmark. He was delighted, however, when the seventy-five-year-old Widmark took him under his wing, telling him stories and amusing quips about his experiences in Hollywood.

In 1989 Neil also appeared in the Hallmark Hall of Fame presentation *Home Fires Burning*, which was based on a novel by Robert Inman. In the movie, Neil played thirteen-year-old Lonnie Tibbetts. In real life he was approaching his sixteenth birthday, but his cherub cheeks and big blue eyes made him look much younger. The movie costars Barnard Hughes and Sada Thompson, who played his grandparents, and Bill Pullman, who played his father, a returning World War II veteran. A reviewer for the *New York Times* said *Home Fires Burning* was "not great drama. In fact, it has some nagging flaws. But . . . [it] has substance and an underlying integrity."[13]

In 1989 Neil guest starred on an episode of the ABC detective drama *B.L. Stryker*, which starred Burt Reynolds as a private investigator in Palm Beach, Florida. One of the best parts of this experience for Neil was getting to meet Reynolds, who had appeared in notable films such as *The Longest Yard* (1974) and *Smokey and the Bandit* (1977). During the filming of the *B.L. Stryker* episode in which Neil appeared, titled "Blues for Buder," Reynolds invited Neil to his house for dinner one night and even gave his sixteen-year-old costar a ride in his private helicopter. To Neil's delight, people walking on the beach below them recognized the helicopter and waved at the two actors.

Neil Patrick Harris was keeping busy and keeping his name and face before the public and, more importantly, directors, producers, and casting agents. With the support of his family, his hard work was already paying off as he embarked on his career as an actor.

Chapter 2

Becoming a Teenage Star

As Neil Patrick Harris approached his sixteenth birthday, he was becoming a sought-after actor. Writers, directors, and producers began asking him to read scripts for both movies and TV shows. One script in particular caught his attention. It was for a half-hour drama-comedy TV series titled *Doogie Howser, M.D.* The title character in the show was a sixteen-year-old genius who was a medical doctor working at a hospital. In between treating patients, however, Doogie, still lived at home with his parents and faced all the typical struggles and trials of an ordinary teenager.

The Hunt for Dr. Howser

The show was created by Steven Bochco, who had created and produced the highly successful dramas *Hill Street Blues* and *L.A. Law*. At first, network executives at ABC doubted that anyone would find a show about a sixteen-year-old doctor believable. Bochco and casting director Robert Harbin, along with David E. Kelley, who wrote the pilot, knew that the success of the show hinged on whomever was cast to play the title role of Doogie Howser. They knew the show would not work unless the main actor could convincingly play the part. They auditioned hundreds of young actors from all over the country. Kelley recalls the difficulty of their search: "We found actors that really got the kid component down, but didn't feel like a doctor. We found other actors that could really handle the doctor part of the equation, but didn't feel like a normal kid to us. It was an exhaustive search."[14]

Steven Bochco

Television veteran Bochco was the producer of Doogie Howser, M.D.

Steven Bochco was born on December 16, 1943, in New York City. He studied at Manhattan's High School of Music and Art and received a bachelor of arts in theater from Carnegie Mellon University in 1966. He worked as a writer, then as a story editor, for the NBC series *Ironside*, *Columbo*, and *McMillan & Wife*. Bochco achieved major success as writer, producer, and cocreater of the NBC cop drama *Hill Street Blues*, which ran from 1981 to 1987. He went on to cocreate and produce the widely acclaimed NBC drama *L.A. Law*, which ran from 1986 to 1994. After making a deal with ABC in 1987 to create and produce ten television series, he formed Steven Bochco Productions, from which came *Doogie Howser, M.D.*, and the very unsuccessful musical *Cop Rock*.

Following the success of *Doogie Howser*, Bochco cocreated the cop drama *NYPD Blue*, which ran from 1993 to 2005. In 1992 Bochco created an animated television series, *Capitol Critters*, for which Neil Patrick Harris provided the voice of the lead character. The enormously creative Bochco had a wide impact on the structure of TV programs; the idea of a large ensemble cast originated with him, as did the practice of having a continuing story line across several episodes of a drama—something previously only done on soap operas.

Harris was among those hundreds of hopefuls who auditioned for the part. Casting director Harbin recalls, "When I first saw Neil, I thought, 'This is our guy.'"[15] Still, however, Harbin, Bochco, and Kelley continued to audition other actors. "We read several hundred kids, including a lot of brats," says Harbin. "But when it was all over, it could only be Neil."[16]

Writer Kelley explains why Neil appealed to the casting team. "He's got an intellect you can actually believe in as he's spewing up the medical jargon, and there's something about him—you care about him as a kid."[17] It was his ability to move back and forth between believable kid and second-year resident that they had been looking for. The hunt for Doogie Howser was over.

Becoming Doogie

To viewers, the baby-faced Neil Patrick Harris seemed like an ideal choice to play the precocious Doogie Howser. Yet because of the exhaustive casting search, he could not claim the part as his own until just two days before the first show began taping. Harris set out to learn as much about his character as he could in those early weeks of taping. Doogie was a child prodigy— someone who is extraordinarily gifted at a very young age—who had a photographic memory. As the show's opening credits reveal, Doogie earned a perfect score on the SAT (a college entrance exam) at age six, completed high school in nine weeks, graduated from Princeton University at age ten, and became a licensed physician at age fourteen. When the show opens, Doogie is in his second year of residency at the fictitious Eastman Medical Center in Los Angeles.

To immerse himself further in the part, Harris read medical textbooks to familiarize himself with some basic terms. He also talked to real doctors, asking them what various things in the script meant. He also asked them how doctors feel about different situations they face in their jobs—for example, treating a young child or responding to an emergency call. In addition, the producers hired a full-time medical consultant to work with Harris and the rest of the cast. From the consultant, Harris learned how to stitch up an incision and various other medical procedures. The consultant also explained to Harris what his lines meant during a surgery scene, for example, and how a real doctor would give orders or deliver diagnoses.

Harris landed the title role on Doogie Howser, M.D., which costarred, from left, Lawrence Pressman, Mitchell Anderson, and Kathryn Layng, in 1989.

Could Doogie Howser Have Been a Real Person?

The notion of a teenage whiz kid with Doogie's lofty achievements seems entirely farfetched to some—but could it happen in real life?

Doogie earned a perfect score on the SAT at age six. Data on six-year-olds taking this rigorous college-entrance exam are nonexistent, but there are statistics on the number of perfect scorers. The SAT is scored differently today than it was when Doogie took it; he scored a 1600, which was the highest possible score on the old scale. According to the book *Perfect 1600 Score* by Tom Fischgrund, only 0.03 percent of the seniors taking the SAT scored a 1600 in any given year.

Doogie graduated from college at age ten, then finished medical school and became a doctor at age fourteen. Only a couple of real-life child prodigies can make similar claims. William James Sidis, a child prodigy in math, set a record in 1909 when he enrolled in Harvard University at age eleven. In 1994 Michael Kearney received a bachelor's degree from the University of South Alabama at age ten, setting a world record for youngest university graduate. The following year Balamurali Ambati became the world's youngest doctor at the age of seventeen.

The pilot episode opens with Doogie taking a driving test for his driver's license on his sixteenth birthday. During the test, a nervous Doogie waits his turn at a stop sign at a completely empty intersection for far too long, until the driving instructor prompts him to go on. Soon, they come upon the scene of a car accident. Doogie's instincts as a doctor spring into action. He pulls the car over to the side of the road, leaps out of the driver's seat, and races toward the accident victim, who is lying in the middle of the road. In his jeans and sneakers, with his loosely fitting overshirt trailing behind him as he runs, Harris makes Doogie totally believable as a teenage boy.

In the next instant, however, Harris makes Doogie totally believable as a teenage doctor: He orders the policemen, who are trying to prevent what they see as a teenage bystander from interfering with the scene of an accident, to unhand him and let him do his job. Harris then orders the policemen to help stabilize the man's neck, delivering his lines rapid-fire and with complete confidence—just as a real doctor would do in an emergency.

A Successful Series

A big reason Harris was believable as a sixteen-year-old, of course, is that he was sixteen in real life. In fact, the fair-haired Harris, who did not even shave yet, actually looked even younger than sixteen, which helped underscore the contrast between his character being

Harris and costar Lisa Dean Ryan appear at the People's Choice Awards in 1990, at which Harris and Doogie Howser, M.D. *were winners.*

a normal teenager on the one hand and a trained doctor on the other. Another parallel existed between Harris and the character he played. Both were adolescents who worked primarily with adults in an adult setting. Harris was the youngest member of the cast; Max Casella, who played Doogie's best friend, Vinnie Delpino, was twenty-two in real life. Even Lisa Dean Ryan, who played Wanda Plenn, Doogie's girlfriend, was a year older than Harris.

The show had one of the highest ratings of any new show during its premiere season, due in large part to Harris's believable performance and affable charm onscreen. *Doogie Howser, M.D.*, ran for four seasons, from 1989 to 1993, on ABC. During the show's run, Harris was nominated for a Golden Globe Award for Best Performance by an Actor in a TV Series. He and the series each won a People's Choice Award after the show's first season. The series won for Favorite New TV Comedy Series, and Harris won for Favorite Male TV Performer in a New TV Series. He also won the Young Artist Award for Best Young Actor Starring in a TV Series three years in a row.

"Like a Circus Sideshow"

In a 1990 interview, Harris explained in simple terms the enormous appeal of his character and the series: "Doogie's a normal kid in an abnormal setting."[18] The same could be said of Harris himself, who spent the majority of his teen years on camera. Over the course of four years, Americans had watched Harris—and Doogie—grow from a sweet, innocent sixteen-year-old to a mature young man of twenty. Harris found the intense scrutiny overwhelming at times, especially because it came during his adolescence, a time when his body was changing and maturing and he was often insecure about his appearance. He describes himself as a late bloomer who was quite self-conscious. Harris found it very hard to feel normal when people would recognize him wherever he went. "It was like a circus sideshow," he recalls of those years. "You'd wear a hat and walk fast, because if someone recognized you, they'd shout your character's name. . . . Everyone was *watching* you, whatever you did."[19]

Despite the changes that fame brought to his life, the teenaged Harris enjoyed finding time to be a normal kid.

TV stardom had changed Harris's life in other ways as well. After he was cast as Doogie, he and his parents moved to a two-room apartment in Century City, California, only a few minutes' drive from the Twentieth Century Fox studio where the show was taped. Ron and Sheila Harris both took time off from their law careers to help their son deal with the tremendous pressures that came along with starring in his own TV series. They also took turns being on the set, since underage actors are required by law to have a parent present during the filming of a movie or TV show. In addition, Harris's parents helped him answer his fan mail; he received up to four hundred letters each week.

School for Harris was also very different now. Because he was sixteen, he was required to spend three hours a day with an on-set tutor. Harris found this difficult at times, because the three hours were not necessarily all in a row. He might study for fifteen minutes at a time between scenes, for example, or talk with his tutor over lunch. In addition, his high school back in Albuquerque, La Cueva, sent his assignments directly to the *Doogie Howser* set, but these were sometimes hard to understand without the classroom instruction that his former classmates received at school. Harris managed to keep up an impressive grade point average nonetheless, graduating from La Cueva High School with honors in 1991 with a 3.8 grade point average.

Despite all the changes, Harris managed to find some time just to be a normal kid. He still hung out with his friends whenever he was back home in Albuquerque. He and Abby Wolf, who was also sixteen, had met in a drama class in Albuquerque and became good friends. They invented an improvisational game that they called "The Psychotic Boyfriend," in which Harris screamed and acted crazy, while Wolf acted like his meek girlfriend. "Neil is very spontaneous,"[20] Wolf explained in a 1990 interview. The two of them liked to walk into video stores and other public places to act out their game, which they thought of as combat theater, and would keep going until one of them burst out laughing.

Another of Harris's favorite hobbies was making short video spoofs of horror films with his buddies in Albuquerque. The amateur videos have titles like *Amish Death Spree* and *Amish Death Spree II*. In both of these, Harris played a deranged

Amish killer who offs his victims in various ways, including stabbing, poisoning, and choking. Neil enjoyed acting in these spoofs and trying to think of more and more ways for his character to kill people.

A Big Shock and a Big Question

Even though Harris enjoyed his time away from the show with his family and friends back in Albuquerque, he loved playing the part of Doogie Howser. Acting had always been his dream, and

Harris became so associated with the role of Doogie Howser that, after the series ended in 1993, he worried whether fans would accept him in other roles.

he was learning a lot about the business. Whenever he had free time on the set, he would visit the sets of other shows and talk with other actors. It was, as Harris later recalled, "a very fast but wonderful education."[21]

Doogie Howser in Pop Culture

Neil Patrick Harris's guest appearance on *Roseanne* is not the only time the character of Doogie Howser has shown up in popular culture. On a 1998 episode of the long-running sitcom *Friends*, a female cast member who is giving birth is shocked by the youthful appearance of her doctor and, assuming he is inexperienced, orders him away with the words, "Shh, Doogie!"[1] Similarly, the comedian Ryan Stiles has made a running joke in his routines out of his slight resemblance to Harris by declaring that he is Doogie Howser, (or, alternatively, as Stiles ages, Doogie Howser's father).

Harris himself has satirized his iconic role several times over the years, most famously in the two *Harold and Kumar* films, in which he appeared as himself. In the 2004 *Harold and Kumar Go to White Castle,* after Harris steals a car from a convenience store, the car's owner tells everyone that Doogie Howser just stole his car. In the film's sequel, *Harold and Kumar Escape from Guantanamo Bay,* Harris declares, "Dude, I was able to perform an appendectomy at age fourteen. ..."[2] Harris further poked fun at his former character in a series of 2008 commercials for Old Spice, claiming to be an expert because he once played a doctor on TV.

1. NBC. "The One Hundredth." *Friends,* season 5, episode 3, October 8, 1998.
2. *Harold and Kumar Escape from Guantanamo Bay.* Directed by Jon Hurwitz and Hayden Schlossberg. Santa Monica, CA: Mandate Pictures, 2008, DVD.

When *Doogie Howser, M.D.*, was canceled in 1993, the cast and crew were caught off guard. The show's ratings had been slipping, and ABC decided it had run its course. The news came as a shock to Harris, who learned the show was canceled in an especially impersonal way: by reading about it in a newspaper. The other members of the cast, as well as the show's fans, were also disappointed. "We never had a final episode,"[22] says Harris. The series ended abruptly with Doogie resigning from the hospital and going to Europe with very little explanation, and viewers were left to wonder what happened next.

Harris now faced the question of what to do with his life. Nearing his twentieth birthday, he had considered college but had not been able to find the time to take away from work to attend classes. He had told himself he would think about college when the show was over. Now that it was, he had the time for college but was concerned that his fame would make it difficult for him to blend in and would be a disruption for others. He also felt that at his age, and with his experience, college would be a step backward in some ways. "I think it would be awkward for me to take Acting 104,"[23] he explained at the time. Harris ultimately decided that what he really wanted was just to keep acting.

That desire led to another big question about his life and career: Would he be forever typecast as Doogie Howser? By the time the series ended, the character of Doogie had already become a part of popular culture. In fact, Harris had even done a guest appearance in 1992 on an episode of the long-running sitcom *Roseanne* in the role of Doogie Howser, complete with his stethoscope and doctor's white coat. Even after the series went off the air, people continued to recognize him in public from his days as the teenage doctor. Ed Alonzo, a close friend of Harris's, recalls a trip the two of them took to Disneyland during the 1990s. Fans would walk up right up to Harris and take his picture without even asking permission. Alonzo also revealed in a 1998 interview that people driving by would honk their car horns at Harris and yell out, "Hey, it's the Doog!"[24]

After the show was canceled, Harris returned to New Mexico to take some time for himself. He had a serious question to ponder. Could he manage to escape from the limitations of his teen idol status after four seasons as Dr. Doogie Howser?

Chapter 3

A Challenging Transition

Harris had made up his mind to continue acting, but in the immediate years following *Doogie Howser,* this proved difficult at times. First, he had to shed his Doogie image and prove to casting agents and producers that he could rise above the role that had thus far defined him. He also faced a second challenge—that of transitioning from child actor to adult actor.

Physically, Harris had already become an adult. Whereas he had been average height with a slight build at sixteen, by the time he turned twenty he had reached his full height of 6 feet 1 inch (185cm) and developed broad shoulders and a more muscular build. He was now tall and graceful and had developed an air of confidence. His physical appearance had changed in other ways, as well. His once fair hair had darkened, and he now tended to keep it cut short or slicked down to control his natural curls. In addition, Harris, long self-conscious about the way his ears stuck out, underwent plastic surgery to have his ears pinned back.

Harris had made the transformation into adult life in other ways as well. He had bought a house in Los Angeles while working on *Doogie Howser*, but when the show was canceled, he moved back to New Mexico and bought an adobe house in Placitas, a small suburb of Albuquerque. While living in Placitas, Harris's career as an adult began to take shape as well, beginning with a series of guest-starring roles and made-for-TV movies that kept his name and face before the public. It would be many years, however, before he would appear in another major theatrical release.

Guest Starring Neil Patrick Harris

Harris first began making guest appearances on other TV shows while he was starring in *Doogie Howser*. In addition to his appearance on *Roseanne* in character as Dr. Howser, audiences watched Harris play a variety of guest-starring roles on other programs. These included an appearance in 1991 on the NBC sitcom *Blossom*, which starred Mayim Bialik as the title character and aired from 1990 to 1995. Harris played a self-absorbed movie star who was billed as "The 'Charming' Derek Slade" in an episode titled "A Rockumentary." This role gave him an opportunity to play a sleazy character that was very different from the earnest Doogie Howser.

In February 1993 he appeared on an episode of the NBC science-fiction series *Quantum Leap*, which starred Scott Bakula. Harris played a college student named Mike Hammond in an episode titled "Return of the Evil Leaper," which was set in 1956. Then in April 1993 came Harris's last guest-starring role before his own show was canceled: He appeared on the CBS mystery series *Murder She Wrote* in April 1993 as Tommy Remsen in an episode titled "Lone Witness." Remsen was a delivery boy who is the only witness to and the prime suspect in a murder. Mystery author and local sleuth Jessica Fletcher, played by Angela Lansbury, befriends Harris's character and helps clear him of suspicion.

Not until 1996 did Harris make another guest appearance on a TV show. This time, he played Howie, a mentally challenged boy, in an episode of the Showtime science-fiction series *The Outer Limits* titled "From Within." The following year he appeared on an episode of the NBC police drama *Homicide: Life on the Street* called "Valentine's Day." Harris played Alan Schack, a graduate student with a menacing demeanor and a violent streak who is suspected of killing his roommate. In these two roles, Harris again broadened his repertoire by playing vastly different types of characters.

In the years since, Harris has continued to make numerous appearances in guest-starring or recurring roles in various TV shows. The roles he has chosen to take have been widely varied,

During and after his run as Doogie Howser, Harris made several guest-starring appearances on other television series that were popular in the early 1990s, including Roseanne, Blossom, Murder She Wrote, and Homicide: Life on the Street.

allowing him to showcase his talent and range as an actor. These guest-starring roles played a large part not only in helping him get offers for movie roles, but also in helping establish him as an adult actor who was making the transition from teen sensation to more mature roles.

Neil Goes Back to the Movies

Harris's continuing work on various TV shows helped secure him larger parts in several made-for-TV movies. The first movie role he took after his own series was canceled was the drama *Sudden Fury* (1993), which is also known as *A Family Torn Apart*. In this NBC TV movie based on a true story, Harris played the part of Brian Hannigan, a teenager who murders his parents to save his brother from mental and physical abuse at the hands of their father. His role in this dark and sober movie offered him the chance to distance himself from the specter of Doogie Howser.

Harris took another dark role in the low-budget film *Animal Room* (1995), which went almost directly to video. He played Arnold Mosk, a tormented high school boy who is relentlessly terrorized by a sadistic bully at his high school, until Arnold takes things into his own hands in the movie's violent conclusion. The movie received only lukewarm reviews and did not generate a very wide viewership.

Although Harris was still being cast as a teenager when he was in his early twenties, he was also beginning to get his first adult roles at this time. In 1994 he played a young adult in the made-for-TV movie *Snowbound: The Jim and Jennifer Stolpa Story*. This movie was based on a real-life crisis faced by a young married couple who became stranded with their infant in the Nevada wilderness during a snowstorm. The movie was generally well liked by viewers, who found Harris believable in the role of a young man whose brash decision to take a shortcut through the countryside in the face of a blizzard came close to costing him his life and that of his young wife and son.

Getting Doogie off His Back

Despite his many guest appearances on TV shows and his costarring parts in TV movies, Harris had yet to be cast in a major feature film. In fact, he had not appeared in a major theatrical release since his debut movie, *Clara's Heart*, in 1988. He believed he was still so strongly associated with his former TV character that audiences—and, more importantly, casting directors—had difficulty seeing him as any other character. Part of the problem, Harris thought, was the nickname given to Douglas Howser, better known as "Doogie." Says Harris, "It's such a funny, stupid name. It sticks."[25]

In an effort to rid himself of Doogie, Harris sought roles he hoped would alter his image and help him make a firm and successful transition to adult roles. His most notable role during this time was as Colonel Carl Jenkins in the science-fiction film *Starship Troopers* (1997). This was the first theatrical release in which Harris had appeared since he was a young teen; it was also the first time he appeared in an adult role in a major film.

Starship Troopers was nominated for the Academy Award for Visual Effects and won a Saturn Award for Best Costumes and Best Special Effects. Film reviewers, however, had mixed opinions about the storyline. Kenneth Turan of the *Los Angeles Times* said the movie was "rigorously one-dimensional and free from even the pretense of intelligence."[26] David Nusair of Reel Film Reviews, however, was kinder in his review, saying the movie "boasts a tongue-in-cheek, downright campy sensibility."[27]

Harris's transition away from Doogie and into more adult roles was sometimes rocky, as evidenced by his appearance in the theatrical release *The Proposition* (1998). The plot concerns a wealthy couple in 1930s Boston named Arthur and Eleanor Barret, played by William Hurt and Madeleine Stowe, who have been unsuccessful in their attempts to conceive a child. Harris played Roger Martin, a young Harvard Law School graduate who is hired to father a child with Eleanor. Even a costarring role by veteran stage and screen actor Kenneth Branagh could not save this movie from receiving low ratings from viewers and critics alike. Charles Tatum, a reviewer for the website eFilmCritic.com, gives this film one star out of five. He complained that the film had an "overly complicated plot" and added, "Harris goes from intelligent law school graduate to overheated sex machine goof in approximately three minutes' screen time."[28]

Harris had a supporting role in the 2000 film *The Next Best Thing*, which starred Madonna, Rupert Everett, and Benjamin Bratt. This comedy-drama did poorly at the box office and was widely panned by critics. Madonna won a Razzie Award for Worst

In 2000, Harris appeared with Madonna, left, and Rupert Everett in the feature film **The Next Best Thing,** *which was mostly panned by critics.*

Actress (Razzie Awards are given out yearly to recognize the worst films and performances), and the movie was nominated for several other Razzies. Harris had better luck with his next feature film, the comedy *Undercover Brother* (2002). In this film he played Lance the Intern, the only white man in an all-black organization, who was hired in order for the firm to avoid charges of racism. This film garnered Harris more attention than the flop *The Next Best Thing*. One reviewer in particular who liked his performance wrote, "Doogie Howser, Neil Patrick Harris, has no trouble playing the square peg in the round hole."[29]

Neil Goes to White Castle

By the turn of the twenty-first century, although he had appeared as a variety of characters on both the big and small screen, Harris had yet to surpass the success he had achieved as Doogie Howser. His popularity with audiences soared, however, when he appeared in the first of the *Harold & Kumar* series of stoner

Harris earned many fans after his raunchy, over-the-top performance in the 2004 comedy **Harold and Kumar Go to White Castle** *and its 2008 sequel.*

comedies in 2004. Called *Harold & Kumar Go to White Castle*, the film stars John Cho and Kal Penn as the title characters. Harris plays a highly fictionalized version of himself, a cocaine-snorting, oversexed hitchhiker who is given a ride by Harold and Kumar, who are on their way to the nearest White Castle restaurant for some hamburgers. When the trio stops at a convenience store to ask for directions, Harris steals Harold's car and drives off into the night.

Normally an actor playing himself onscreen would be listed in the credits as "Himself." But Harris asked instead for the credits to read "Neil Patrick Harris as Neil Patrick Harris." He wanted to disassociate himself from the over-the-top exploits of the fictionalized version of himself in the movie. "I didn't want it to seem like I was saying, 'Hey, America, I'm really like this!'"[30] Harris explains.

The film grossed nearly $5.5 million during its opening weekend in the United States and Canada. The movie was well received by audiences and reviewers alike. Famed film critic Roger Ebert gave it three stars out of four, and Brian McKay of eFilmCritic. com commented, "It's what a stoner comedy should be. It's what a buddy comedy should be." McKay added that Harris's cameo appearance "steals the movie hands-down."[31]

Harris appeared as himself again in the 2008 sequel to *White Castle*, called *Harold & Kumar Escape from Guantanamo Bay*. The plot involves Harold and Kumar trying to get to Amsterdam to find Maria, Harold's love interest. Kumar is mistaken for a terrorist, however, and the pair are sent to Guantanamo Bay detention camp. Audiences and reviewers had mixed reactions to the movie, and many thought it was not as funny as the original. A reviewer for British newspaper the *Guardian* called the storyline "total nonsense" but also noted that during the screening he attended, "even the opening credits were wildly applauded, and much of the dialogue was inaudible over the laughter."[32]

A third installment, titled *A Very Harold & Kumar Christmas*, came out in November 2011. In this film Harold and Kumar roam New York City in search of the perfect Christmas tree after accidentally burning down the beloved tree of Harold's father-in-law. For this film, which was shot in 3-D, Harris reprised his role as the drug-crazed and highly unpredictable former child star. Thanks largely to the popularity of the *Harold & Kumar* films, Harris was beginning to make a comeback.

Neil Finds a New Series

While he was appearing in movies, Harris kept an open mind about returning to TV as a regular on a series. From 1999 to 2000, he starred with Tony Shalhoub in the short-lived NBC sitcom *Stark Raving Mad*. Harris played the somewhat neurotic editor of Shalhoub's horror novel–writing character. The series lasted only twenty-two episodes before being canceled.

Harris next auditioned for a part in the science-fiction TV series *Firefly*, which premiered on Fox in September 2002 but was canceled after only eleven episodes were aired. The part Harris

Harris was cast as serial womanizer Barney Stinson on the CBS comedy How I Met Your Mother *in 2005.*

The Cast of *How I Met Your Mother*

In addition to Neil Patrick Harris, the ensemble cast of *How I Met Your Mother* includes four other talented actors. Before his leading role as architect Ted Mosby, Josh Radnor made guest appearances on shows such as *Law & Order* and *ER*. He also appeared alongside Harris onstage in a 2004 production of *The Paris Letter*. He made his writing and directing debut for the film *Happythankyoumoreplease*, which won the 2010 Sundance Film Festival Audience Award. Alyson Hannigan, who plays Lily Aldrin, is also known for her roles on TV's *Buffy the Vampire Slayer* and in the *American Pie* films.

Jason Segel plays Marshall Eriksen, Lily's husband. He previously appeared on the NBC series *Freaks and Geeks* and had a recurring role on the CBS drama *CSI: Crime Scene Investigation*. Segel wrote and starred in the 2008 film *Forgetting Sarah Marshall*, which was nominated for five Teen Choice Awards. Cobie Smulders plays Canadian television reporter Robin Scherbatsky. She has guest starred in several TV shows, including *Jeremiah* and *Smallville*. She had a recurring role on the Showtime drama *The L Word* before being cast as Robin.

Jason Segel, left, Alyson Hannigan, Josh Radnor, Cobie Smulders, and Harris star in How I Met Your Mother.

tried out for, Dr. Simon Tam, went instead to Sean Maher. Harris was disappointed, but he continued to look at other possibilities that might bring him back to TV on a regular basis.

Then in 2005 Harris's career reached a turning point when he auditioned for the part of Barney Stinson in a new CBS series called *How I Met Your Mother*. He initially did not think he would get the part, because the producers had someone very different in mind to play Barney. However, after seeing Harris's wild performance in *Harold & Kumar Go to White Castle*, the producers decided that a toned-down version of that performance would make for a perfect Barney Stinson. Harris says of his audition, "I went in with no expectations at all. . . . I just went in and kind of made an ass of myself, and sure enough, that's what they wanted."[33]

The Bro Code

The Bro Code is the first in a series of books "written by" Harris's *How I Met Your Mother* character, Barney Stinson. In reality, the books were written by one of the show's writers, Matt Kuhn. The books contain a collection of rules that govern how bros (guys and their guy friends) should interact with each other, as well as with the opposite sex. At the end of each episode of the show, a placard on the screen briefly shows one of these humorous bro codes.

The book offers bros advice on a variety of topics. These include guidelines for dating, such as the required wait time before calling a woman after obtaining her phone number (ninety-six hours). There are also codes that govern ways to appear more manly; for example, never wearing a cell phone on a belt clip. Similarly, a bro will not ask for directions or admit he cannot drive a car with a stick shift. The most common type of rules are those that pertain to a bro's relationship with other bros. For example, bros are not expected to remember each other's birthdays, but are expected to post bail for one another—unless, of course, the bail is really, really expensive.

On the show, Barney is a serial womanizer who never calls women back after sleeping with them and oftentimes does not even know their names. A confirmed bachelor, he has commitment issues and cringes at the thought of marriage. Harris is very different from Barney, but is able to play him convincingly. The show's executive producer, Carter Bays, says, "The thing Neil had that put him over the top is he is just this person you naturally like. It allows us to go places with Barney that, coming from anyone else, you'd think, 'What a despicable human being!'"[34]

The character of Barney was originally intended to be a supporting player, a sidekick of the main character, Ted. But largely due to Harris's skills and the ease with which he slips into the character, Barney has become not only a bigger part of the show, but also a part of pop culture. In fact, Barney is so popular among fans that he inspired a spinoff book, *The Bro Code*, which gives credit to Barney Stinson as its primary author.

How I Met Your Mother has earned high ratings and received critical acclaim. It has won five Emmy Awards. For his role as Barney Stinson, Harris has been nominated four times for the Primetime Emmy Award for Outstanding Supporting Actor in a Comedy Series. Harris himself says that of all his projects, his favorite has been *How I Met Your Mother*.

A Long Way from Doogie

Harris has come a long way since his days as the teenage doctor, and yet it is a role he will never entirely escape. Nor, it seems, would he want to. During a 2006 appearance on CBS's *The Early Show*, interviewer Julie Chen asked him to answer a true-or-false question: Did he hate his Doogie Howser role? Harris reacted with genuine surprise and replied "False!" He gave Chen a puzzled look and said, "That's an odd question."[35] He has stressed in several interviews that he embraces his work on the iconic TV series as a part of who he is. And, if he is forever associated with the role he played in his late teens, that would be just fine with Harris.

Chapter 4

Onstage and Behind the Mic

In addition to his appearances on television and in movies, Neil Patrick Harris has also appeared in several live theater productions. It is mainly these appearances on the stage, which require him to use and sharpen a different set of acting skills, that have allowed him to grow as a performer. Harris, who has always been interested in the theater, began acting onstage professionally in the mid-1990s after *Doogie Howser* was canceled. He has appeared onstage in both dramatic and musical roles. Always ready to lend his talents and his voice to a production, Harris has also done voice-over work on several animated TV shows and movies. His voice can be heard in a number of other places as well, including several audiobooks for children and adults.

"A Lifelong Dream"

Harris got his first taste of professional live theater in Albuquerque as a kid, and has been smitten ever since. Soon after his first TV series was canceled, he decided to pursue stage work in addition to his TV appearances. In a 1996 interview, Harris explained, "Starring in a live theatrical show is a lifelong dream of mine."[36]

"A *Huge* Theater Fan"

As a theater performer and a fan, Harris was inspired to support the Albuquerque theater group where he got his start after a fire.

Neil Patrick Harris appeared in many community theater productions as a teen, including a stint as Peter Pan at Albuquerque's Musical Theatre Southwest in 1988. These experiences deeply affected Harris, who declares, "I am a *huge* theater fan." So when an arsonist set fire to one of the buildings belonging to the Musical Theatre Southwest in May 2010, Harris took it very personally.

The fire completely destroyed a warehouse that was used as rehearsal space and which housed costumes, sets, and props. Although no one was injured, the theater lost its entire stock of 150,000 costumes, all its props, and archives dating back fifty years, including photographs, videos, and posters of past productions. The theater asked the Albuquerque community for donations such as clothing racks, hangers, folding tables and chairs, tools, building materials, sewing machines, costuming supplies, and vintage clothing from the 1940s and 1950s.

Harris decided he had to do something for the theater that had helped launch his career onstage. He and his family pitched in by holding a fund-raiser at their Albuquerque restaurant, Perennials, which is currently run by Neil's older brother, Brian. One hundred patrons paid $150 per plate at a special dinner that included musical performances, and the Harris family raised $15,000 to help the theater get back on its feet.

Quoted in Susan King. "Profile: Miles from Doogie." *Los Angeles Times*, November 21, 1993. http://articles.latimes.com/1993-11-21/news/tv-59138_1_doogie-howser.

He got his chance in the dark comedy *Luck, Pluck & Virtue*. The play is playwright and director James Lapine's adaptation of the novel *A Cool Million* by Nathanael West. Harris made his New York stage debut in the fall of 1994. He played Lester Price, a young man who sets out to help save his mother's home from foreclosure but is met by a series of increasingly awful misfortunes. Audiences and theater critics had mixed reactions to the play, but most agreed that Harris's performance was very good. One reviewer for *Newsday* found the play bleak and predictable, but said, "Harris is perfectly cast as Lester Price."[37]

Other dramatic roles followed his turn as Price. In 1998 he appeared in a production of *Romeo and Juliet* at San Diego's Old Globe Theatre, playing Romeo with what one reviewer described as "casual confidence."[38] Harris also appeared in the Culver City, California, production of Jon Robin Baitz's *The Paris Letter* in 2004 (with future *How I Met Your Mother* costar Josh Radnor) and in a Los Angeles production of the Arthur Miller drama *All My Sons* in 2006.

Fulfilling a Fantasy

As much as he was enjoying himself in dramatic parts onstage, Harris had another deep desire: to appear in a musical. In 1996, while he was in Boston filming the movie *The Proposition*, he heard that the rock opera *Rent* was coming to town. With music and lyrics by Jonathan Larson (who had died suddenly of a brain aneurism the morning of the opera's off-Broadway premiere in 1996), *Rent* revolves around a group of young actors and musicians dealing with HIV/AIDS in New York's Lower East Side.

Harris was already a huge fan of the Pulitzer and Tony Award–winning musical, so he started hanging out with the cast in Boston, who encouraged him to audition for the upcoming West Coast production. Although Harris had no previous dance training and only a few singing lessons, he auditioned for director Michael Grief. "I had heard wildly enthusiastic things about Neil from a number of people I knew and trusted," recalls Greif. Still, he was wary, because that praise was for Harris's acting, and *Rent* was a

Harris bleached his hair blond for a role in the stage musical Rent, *in which he debuted in 1997.*

musical. Greif was pleasantly surprised when Harris auditioned and recalls, "He came in to sing, and he sang terrifically."[39]

Harris won the part of aspiring filmmaker Mark Cohen, and in July 1997 made his musical stage debut at the La Jolla Playhouse in San Diego. "It was like fulfilling my rock-star fantasy,"[40] he said at the time. Harris bleached his hair blond and painted his nails black for the role. He felt like he had to prove himself every night onstage, because people still associated him with the role of the squeaky-clean Doogie Howser. His performance, though, was well received by audiences and reviewers alike. A *Los Angeles Times* theater critic called his appearance in *Rent* "a mighty stroke of good casting" and added, "Harris not only has a winsome voice, he's lanky and light on his feet."[41]

"The Exceptionally Tender Mr. Harris"

Numerous other musical performances followed Harris's successful turn in *Rent*. He played Tobias Ragg in several different concert performances of Stephen Sondheim's *Sweeney Todd*. His first appearance in this musical thriller, along with Kelsey Grammar and Christine Baranski, was in 1999 at Los Angeles's Ahmanson Theatre. Harris reprised his role as Ragg in 2000 at Lincoln Center in New York. This performance was recorded and released as a deluxe two-CD set called *Sweeney Todd: Live in Concert*. Harris appeared as Ragg again in San Francisco in 2001 with the San Francisco Symphony. This production was taped and broadcast on PBS and later released on DVD. His performance in *Sweeney Todd* was highly praised. Peter Marks of the *New York Times* wrote that "the exceptionally tender Mr. Harris, best known and criminally underemployed as television's Doogie Howser, [was] nothing less than breathtaking."[42]

In 2002 Harris made his Broadway debut in *Proof* alongside Anne Heche. This Pulitzer and Tony Award–winning play by David Auburn centers on Catherine, a mathematical genius who may or may not be mentally unstable. Harris played the part of Hal, who becomes romantically involved with Catherine. Bruce Weber, a reviewer for the *New York Times*, called the play "a crisp crowd pleaser." He had a less glowing assessment of Harris's performance, however, writing that Harris "is a little uncertain and seems to be playing by rote" but that he manages to settle into the role and portray "the gentleness, decency and self-awareness in Hal."[43]

Harris appears in the theater in which he starred as the Emcee in a revival of the stage musical Cabaret *in 2003.*

Harris appeared on Broadway again in 2003 as the Emcee in a revival of *Cabaret*, which won the Tony Award for Best Revival of a Musical. Based on a book by Joe Masteroff, *Cabaret* debuted on Broadway in 1966 and became a hit 1972 film starring Liza Minnelli. *Cabaret* is set in a seedy nightclub in Berlin in 1931. Harris took over the role of Emcee from veteran stage and screen actor Alan Cumming (the role has also been played onstage by John Stamos, Raul Esparza, Adam Pascal, and Jon Secada). Harris received critical acclaim for his performance, and GuestStarCasting.com named him the top-drawing headliner in the role of the Emcee.

Harris's earlier performance in *Sweeney Todd* had impressed Stephen Sondheim, who asked Harris to appear in another of his productions. In 2004 Harris performed in a Broadway revival of Sondheim's Tony Award–winning *Assassins*. This dark and inventive musical is about the real actions and imagined interactions of the murderers or would-be murderers of U.S. presidents. Harris played a dual role as the Balladeer (the narrator) and as Lee Harvey Oswald. He received excellent reviews for his performance, including this one from the *New York Times*: "All cast members are in good voice, especially Neil Patrick Harris who, if you have not seen him onstage will surprise and really impress you."[44]

Harris continued to impress audiences and reviewers in other stage appearances, including the London production of *Tick, Tick . . . BOOM!* in 2005. The following year he appeared in the title role of *Amadeus* at the Hollywood Bowl. More recently, Harris appeared in a limited-run revival of another Sondheim musical, *Company*, in 2011. This work centers around Bobby, a single man with commitment issues; his numerous girlfriends; and his circle of friends—five married couples. Harris headed an all-star cast that included Stephen Colbert, Jon Cryer, Martha Plimpton, and Anika Noni Rose. A filmed performance of the musical debuted in movie theaters in June 2011. In addition, the cast performed live at the *65th Annual Tony Awards* in June 2011, singing "Side by Side by Side/What Would We Do Without You?"

In addition to the critical acclaim he received for his onstage performances in musicals, Harris was also well received when he guest starred in a part written specifically for him on an episode of the Fox comedy-drama *Glee* in 2010. In the episode, Harris sang the Aerosmith classic song "Dream On." For this performance, he won the Emmy Award for Outstanding Guest Performance by a Male Actor in a Comedy Series.

A Degree in Horrible

An interesting and highly unusual project came Harris's way in 2008. Writer and director Joss Whedon came up with the idea to write and produce a web series. He and his two brothers, writer Zack Whedon and composer Jed Whedon, along with actress Maurissa Tancharoen, wrote a script for a campy musical they decided to title *Dr. Horrible's Sing-Along Blog*. Harris starred in the title role, alongside Felicia Day as Penny, his love interest, and Nathan Fillion as Captain Hammer, his archenemy. The story, told in three acts, follows the lovesick Billy as he pines away for Penny. Unknown to Penny, Billy has an alter ego: Dr. Horrible, an aspiring mad scientist trying to get into the Evil League of Evil.

Dr. Horrible's Sing-Along Blog was a big hit with online audiences and won a number of awards. These included a Hulu Award for Best Web Original; a Hugo Award for Best Dramatic Presentation, Short Form; a People's Choice Award for Best Internet Phenomenon; and a Creative Arts Emmy Award for Outstanding Special Class. The web production also won big at the first annual Streamy Awards in 2009. (Popularly known as the Streamys, these are presented by the International Academy of Web Television to recognize excellence in web television production). *Dr. Horrible's Sing-Along Blog* won four Streamys: Audience Choice Award for Best Web Series, Best Directing for a Comedy Web Series, Best Writing for a Comedy Web Series, and Best Male Actor in a Comedy Web Series. When Harris won the best male actor Streamy for his portrayal of Dr. Horrible, he said in his acceptance speech that the web musical was "so fantastically fun to make."[45]

Giving Voice to Others

Not only has Harris appeared in numerous musical productions of various sorts, he has also given voice to animated features on TV and in the movies. Harris has been lending his voice to

Harris has voiced several animated characters on television and in film, including Steve the monkey in the 2009 movie **Cloudy with a Chance of Meatballs.**

animated characters since 1991, when he guest starred on an episode of *The Simpsons*. From 1992 to 1995 he lent his voice to the animated series *Capitol Critters*, giving life to a young mouse named Max who leaves his home in the country after his family is wiped out by an exterminator and travels to Washington, D.C. The series was produced by Steven Bochco (who had created and produced *Doogie Howser*) and Hanna-Barbera Productions in association with 20th Century Fox Television for ABC.

Harris lent his voice to superhero Spider-Man in the 2003 MTV series *Spider-Man: The New Animated Series*, which ran for one season. His voice is also featured in the 2009 family comedy *Cloudy with a Chance of Meatballs*, a computer-animated film

Neil the Murderer

In October 1991 an eighteen-year-old Neil Patrick Harris guest starred on the Fox network's long-running animated sitcom *The Simpsons*. In an episode titled "Bart the Murderer," Bart Simpson lands in some trouble when members of the local Mafia frame him for the murder of Bart's principal, Seymour Skinner. Eventually, when it is discovered that Skinner is not actually dead but rather has been trapped beneath a huge pile of old newspapers in his garage for the past week, Bart is cleared of the charges. In the meantime, however, the Simpson family watches a fake documentary on TV titled *Blood on the Blackboard: The Bart Simpson Story*. Harris played himself providing the voice of Bart in this comically inaccurate depiction of Bart's life and encounters with the Mafia.

The episode "Bart the Murderer" was Fox's highest-rated show the week it aired. It has another claim to fame, however. Exclaims Harris proudly, "I am the ONLY other person who has played Bart on *The Simpsons*."

Quoted in *Oldsmobile Celebrity Circle*. "Neil Patrick Harris Chats on AOL." Transcript, America Online, July 18, 1996. http://chloe74.tripod.com/articles/article5.html.

based on the children's book by Judi and Ron Barrett. Harris provided the voice for Steve, the Flint family's pet monkey, who communicates using a handheld monkey thought translator. In 2010 he provided the voice of yet another animal, Lou the beagle, in the live-action comedy *Cats & Dogs: The Revenge of Kitty Galore*.

In 2009 Harris appeared in a mostly singing part in a musical episode of the animated series *Batman: The Brave and the Bold* on Cartoon Network, providing the voice of the villain known as Music Meister. In 2010 he made another appearance in a Batman feature, providing the voice for the adult Dick Grayson (the true identity of Nightwing) in the animated 2010 film *Batman: Under the Red Hood*.

The Ubiquitous Voice of Neil Patrick Harris

Harris's voice seems to be just about everywhere. He has done voice-overs for several video games, including *Saints Row 2*, *Rock of the Dead*, and *Eat Lead: The Return of Matt Hazard*. In 2010 he once again provided a voice for Spider-Man, this time for the video game *Spider-Man: Shattered Dimensions*. Harris says he is not sure why he was asked twice to provide the voice of this super-hero but says maybe it was because he has a young-sounding voice. Or, as he jokes: "Maybe I'm just good at going 'Uhh,' 'Ahh,' 'Oww.'"[46] Harris has done such extensive voice work that he can even be heard in the recording of the safety guidelines for the roller coaster called California Screamin' at the Disney California Adventure theme park in Anaheim.

Harris has also narrated a number of audiobooks. These include several children's books by Beverly Cleary, such as *Henry Huggins* (2001), *Henry and the Clubhouse* (2006), and *Henry and the Paper Route* (2006). Other children's audiobooks narrated by Harris include *Slake's Limbo* (2000) by Felice Holman, *A Coyote's in the House* (2004) by Elmore Leonard, *A Very Marley Christmas* (2008) by John Grogan, and *The Lump of Coal* (2008) by Lemony Snicket. Harris has also narrated adult novels, including the murder mystery *The Hunt Club* (1998) by Bret Lott and the thriller *Long Lost* (2002) by David Morrell.

In the theater and behind the scenes, Neil Patrick Harris has proved himself as a hardworking and multifaceted actor with a wide range of talents. He has fulfilled a lifelong dream of performing in both dramatic and musical stage roles and, even more fulfilling for him, of appearing on Broadway. "I enjoy theater much more than TV," says Harris. "The dynamic of the live audience is utterly unique."[47] He has kept his name, his face, and his voice in the public through his many varied pursuits—and has managed to have a lot of fun doing so.

Chapter 5

Shattering the Glass Closet

A large part of Neil Patrick Harris's identity is his sexual orientation, and the fact that he is an openly gay actor puts him in a unique situation. Not many other openly gay male actors have enjoyed the degree of commercial success Harris has. In addition, his willingness to be open about his homosexuality has made him a role model to others who have struggled with their own sexual identity. Harris has also been outspoken in his support of gay causes. Professionally and personally, he remains very satisfied with his life.

A Big Realization

Harris first met other homosexuals when as a young teen he went to Hollywood to make his first movie appearances. Meeting gay adults made him think about his own sexuality. He started to wonder whether he himself might be gay when he was about fourteen years old. At first he was resistant to this idea. It was not the way he had been brought up, after all, and no one else in his family was known to be gay. Moreover, in the late 1980s when he first began to question his own sexuality, being gay was even more looked down on in society than it is today.

Harris explored his feelings for several years and in various ways, trying to discover his own deepest truths. He dated many

Harris steps out with date with actress Robyn Lively, left, in 1993. After several relationships with women, he eventually came to terms with his homosexuality.

different girls and managed for a long time to avoid any sexual activity, usually by casting himself as the life of the party, the guy who is cute and witty, but not sexual. Finally, as he approached adulthood, he became sexually intimate with several different women. By the time he reached his early twenties, he knew he could no longer deny who he was. While dating Christine Taylor, a young actress, Harris realized he was not at all physically attracted to her. He decided that if he was attracted to men and did not feel any sparks with a woman as beautiful and sweet as Taylor that definitely meant he was gay.

Harris's first encounter with another man was at age twenty-four, with a fellow cast member in *Rent*. Still, however, he kept his private life discreet. At the time, he was still afraid of being found out. Because he was so easily recognized as Doogie Howser, he felt he was unable to be open about who he was without the whole world knowing about it.

Living in a Glass Closet

Despite his fears of being judged negatively for his homosexuality, Harris gradually came out privately to his family and friends in the mid-1990s. He need not have worried; everyone was very supportive of him and praised him for his courage in telling them. Many members of his family, as well as several friends, said they already knew that he was gay.

Although his family and friends were very accepting of the news, Harris was not ready to come out publicly yet. During interviews, in answering questions about his romantic life, he never lied or made up a fake girlfriend, but he did skirt the issue by answering with carefully chosen words that were not gender specific. For example, rather than referring to the men he had dated, he would instead refer to the people he had dated. Or he might describe a relationship with a specific man phrasing things in the plural—substituting "we went to a play," for example, rather than "he and I went to a play."

Keeping one's sexuality a secret is commonly called living in "the closet." The situation of celebrities being out to their friends and family, but keeping their sexual orientation a secret from the press and public, is sometimes called living in "the glass closet." Harris did a good job of keeping his sexuality private: He managed to stay inside the glass closet for about a decade. He never tried to hide his sexual orientation from producers, casting directors, and fellow actors, but when it came to the press and the public at large, that was another story. He simply was not ready to make the most intimate details of his private life public.

Finding Love

In 2003, while Harris was appearing on Broadway in *Cabaret*, he met fellow actor David Burtka, who was appearing on Broadway in *Gypsy*. The two met through a mutual female friend, and went on their first date in 2004. It did not take long for them to fall in love.

Unlike Harris, who has done extensive work in TV and in movies, Burtka is primarily a stage actor. He has never been guarded about his sexuality the way Harris was, because gay artists have long been accepted in the theater world. Harris, however, had to worry about the effect it would have on the TV and movie side of his career if he came out publicly. By the time the two of them had dated for about a year and were getting serious, Harris had been cast in *How I Met Your Mother*. Although Harris was very upfront with the show's producers and cast (and in fact Burtka accompanied him to the set from time to time), their relationship was not publicized.

All of that began to change, however, when Burtka guest starred on an episode of *How I Met Your Mother* in May 2006. Burtka played Scooter, the former high school boyfriend of one of the female characters on the show. A few months later, a rumor appeared in print that Burtka had gotten the part on the show because he and Harris were in a romantic relationship. Although the blurb printed on Canada.com was brief, only a paragraph long, the pressure on Harris to publicly acknowledge his sexual orientation began to mount.

Theater actor David Burtka appears at a Tony Awards event in 2006. He and Harris began dating in 2004.

David Burtka

Neil Patrick Harris's partner, David Burtka, was born in Dearborn, Michigan, on May 29, 1975. He graduated from Plymouth-Salem High School in Canton, Michigan, and attended the University of Michigan, graduating with a bachelor of fine arts degree. He also studied acting at Michigan's Interlochen

Burtka, left, makes a curtain call with his The Play About the Baby *costars in 2001.*

Center for the Arts and received further training at Manhattan's William Esper Studio, a school for the performing arts.

In 2001 Burtka appeared in the off-Broadway production of *The Play About the Baby*, playing the part of "The Boy," a role that won him the Clarence Derwent Award for most promising male performer. In 2003 Burtka made his Broadway debut playing the part of Tulsa in *Gypsy*. He went on to appear in the play *The Opposite Sex* in 2004. Burtka has also made several TV appearances, including guest appearances on *The West Wing*, *Crossing Jordan*, and *How I Met Your Mother*.

Burtka recently decided to give up acting altogether in 2010 and focus on his career as a chef. He holds a degree from Le Cordon Bleu College of Culinary Arts in Pasadena, California. In 2010 he cofounded a catering company in Los Angeles called Gourmet M.D.

Neil Comes Out

After the story on Canada.com appeared, Harris received much attention in the tabloids as well as on the Internet. Bloggers and the press alike accused him of hiding his sexuality. One celebrity

Burtka, left, and Harris make their first public appearance as a couple on the red carpet of the 2007 Emmy Awards.

gossip blogger, Perez Hilton, was particularly relentless in his calls for Harris to out himself publicly. Hilton, who is himself openly gay, actively goes after celebrities whom he accuses of being closeted, such as former *NSYNC member Lance Bass. After much badgering by Hilton and others in the press, Bass came out publicly in July 2006.

Now Hilton set his sights on Neil Patrick Harris, asking people to send in any photos of Harris in public with other men, particularly if they were embracing or otherwise physically expressing affection. In November 2006 Harris's publicist responded to Hilton's crusade by issuing a statement denying that Harris was gay. The following day, however, Harris decided to come out publicly. He made an exclusive statement to *People* magazine, which read in part: "I am happy to dispel any rumors or misconceptions and am quite proud to say that I am a very content gay man living my life to the fullest."[48] The following summer Harris and Burtka moved in together, in a house Harris had bought in Studio City, California. They made their first appearance as an openly gay couple at the Emmy Awards show in September 2007.

"A Truly Elegant Trick"

Harris worried at first about public reaction to his announcement and how it would affect his career. When comedian and actress Ellen DeGeneres had come out in 1997, controversy over the issue led to the end of her self-titled TV sitcom and sent her career into a nosedive for several years. But society had become more accepting of gay and lesbian performers in the decade since DeGeneres publicly acknowledged she was gay, and more stars were coming out of the closet. Yet, as one writer for New York magazine points out, coming out can be harder on male actors, who risk losing lead roles as a result: "Straight women won't be able to fantasize about him; straight men won't be able to relate."[49]

Howard Bragman, a public relations specialist, agrees that coming out is a big deal for a male TV or film actor, because

Jennifer Lopez made a guest-starring appearance on
How I Met Your Mother *in 2010 as woman out to seduce*
Harris's character Barney.

there is still a double standard in Hollywood—a straight actor can play a gay character in a movie, for example, but audiences are reluctant to accept a gay actor playing a straight character. This conundrum was especially an issue for Harris, who plays not just a straight character, but a highly sexualized one. He was concerned that his coming out could affect the show's ratings if the audience no longer found him, as a gay actor, credible in the role of Barney Stinson, a serial womanizer. As Bragman puts it, "Neil Patrick Harris is . . . playing not just a heterosexual but an aggressively heterosexual man on his show."[50]

Yet Harris has not only weathered the potentially disastrous experience of coming out, he has thrived. "As a celebrity, Harris has managed to pull off a truly elegant trick, something no male actor has done to date—he has come out as gay without stunting his career," observed Emily Nussbaum in *New York* magazine. "Instead, his fame has spiked upward."[51] The cast and crew of *How I Met Your Mother* were among the many people who supported him. Said Carter Bays, one of the creators of the show, "Being gay isn't something Neil has ever hidden from anyone who knows him. He's proud of who he is, and should be—he's . . . a terrific guy."[52]

The public has been very accepting of him as well, treating the issue of his sexual orientation as, in Harris's view, a nonissue. This is in part due, no doubt, to his personal charm and his considerable ability to make his characters come across as real human beings. He said of the fact that the public was so accepting of him, "I think that speaks well to our society today."[53] Not only has Harris's career not come to a standstill, he has actually become even more famous and in demand as a performer in the years since he came out. In fact, he played a married father in *The Best and the Brightest*, a 2010 film in which a young couple is trying to get their five-year-old daughter into a good kindergarten. And Bragman, who credits actors such as Harris with helping audiences accept gay men in straight roles, says, "It's things like [Harris playing straight parts] that are changing the dialogue and changing people's mindset, but we still have hurdles to overcome."[54]

Here Come the Twins

In *The Best and the Brightest*, Harris plays a dad. In real life, he had wanted to become a parent for several years. After he and Burtka had been together for more than six years, they decided to start a family. Together they adopted fraternal twins, a boy and a girl, born via a surrogate mother on October 12, 2010. Harris and Burtka are each the biological father of one twin, named Gideon Scott and Harper Grace. Two eggs were implanted in the surrogate mother; one had been fertilized with Harris's sperm and the other with Burtka's. Harris and Burtka have not made public which of them is the biological father of which baby.

Harris, who is "Papa," and Burtka, who is "Daddy," say that becoming parents is an experience that has filled both of them with awe. Burtka says that when he and Harris held the newborns in the delivery room shortly after the twins' birth, the two men both felt "just absolute joy." He also expressed the wonder the two of them felt about the birth of their twins: "We had two babies that we made. With help."[55]

Burtka and Harris stayed at the hospital every night until the twins came home, bottle feeding, burping, and changing diapers. The day they brought the twins home, Harris wrote on his Twitter page, "Gideon Scott and Harper Grace entered the Burtka-Harris fold. All of us are happy, healthy, tired, and a little pukey."[56]

Shortly after the twins' birth, the family moved to a new home in Hollywood Hills. The house is very kid friendly and includes a nursery decorated with Disney characters. They also hired a nanny to help them with the babies. The nanny helped get the infants on the same sleeping and eating schedule, a development the doting dads especially appreciate.

New parents Harris and Burtka began wearing rings in 2006, although they have not yet married. They each wear their ring on the right hand, rather than the left, which is the customary hand for a wedding ring. In June 2011, with the legalization of gay marriage in New York State (where Harris and Burtka also reside), they announced their intentions via Twitter to tie the

After six years together, Harris and Burtka welcomed twins born via a surrogate mother in October 2010.

"Two Lucky Babies"

After the birth of their twins, new dads Neil Patrick Harris and David Burtka paid a visit to Harris's costar Alyson Hannigan and her husband, Alexis Denisof, for parenting advice. Hannigan and Denisof, the parents of a then nineteen-month-old daughter named Satyana, were happy to oblige. They gave Harris and Burtka a list of their favorite baby products and discussed the challenges posed by the first six weeks of parenting. They explained how to figure out what each kind of crying means as well as finding a schedule that works best for the baby. Hannigan says that Harris and Burtka will be great parents and that Harris's creativity will come in handy. For example, he has made up a song for Hannigan's daughter that the little girl adores. Says Hannigan, "Those are going to be two lucky babies."

Quoted in Paul Chi. "Alyson Hannigan Is So Excited Neil Patrick Harris Is a New Dad." *People*, October 16, 2010. www.people.com/people/article/0,,20434923,00.html.

knot. "I've already [proposed], he said yes!" tweeted Burtka. He added, "He proposed to me as well. I said yes!"[57] Harris confided that the engagement is not actually recent, however. "David and I did propose to each other, but over five years ago!" he tweeted. "We've been wearing engagement rings for ages, waiting for an available date."[58] When they do marry, they will move the rings to their left hands.

An Outspoken Role Model

For Harris, the issue of marriage is not just personal; it is also political, and he has used his celebrity to offer support for gay marriage and other gay rights causes. For example, just hours before the resolution passed in New York legalizing gay marriage, he

An active supporter of gay rights causes, Harris was a featured speaker at the Democratic National Committee's Lesbian Gay Bisexual Transgender Leadership Gala in June 2011.

wrote on his Twitter page: "I'd sure love to get married. Please, NY Senate, vote in favor of marriage equality today. My family would really appreciate it." A few hours later, an ecstatic Harris wrote, "It PASSED! Marriage equality in NY!! Yes!! Progress!! Thank you everyone who worked so hard on this!! A historic night!"[59]

Harris also spoke out against the military's Don't Ask, Don't Tell policy on his personal Twitter page, writing: "The Senate just rejected the repeal for Don't Ask, Don't Tell, 57-40. I'm stunned, and more upset than I thought I would be."[60] He followed up this post nine days later with the announcement: "Don't Ask, Don't Tell REPEALED! So proud of Congress for making the right decision. Now all soldiers can serve with integrity. A great day."[61]

Harris has helped raise funds for the Trevor Project, which provides a crisis prevention hotline and educational outreach programs for gay youth. He also created a 2010 MTV public service announcement aimed at gay teens. The announcement aired in light of a cluster of four teen suicides that year that were provoked by antigay bullying. He tells teens that life gets better as one gets older because individuals become more valued than a group. He also urges victims of bullying to not hurt themselves and tells them to "stand tall and be proud of who you are."[62]

Harris has followed his own advice and proved himself an excellent role model. "I've been grateful and relieved we live in a world where I don't have to feel innate shame for who I choose to fall in love with," he says. He even feels like coming out of the closet has made him a better actor, because being open about his homosexuality has "allowed me to stand tall, and when you're standing tall, I think you perform better."[63] His acceptance of himself for who he is, and the way he lives his life, makes him someone that all young people, gay or straight, male or female, can look up to. It is also part of what makes him so appealing in his many roles as a performer.

Chapter 6

Neil Patrick Harris as Neil Patrick Harris

Neil Patrick Harris was once primarily known as only one character, teenage doctor Doogie Howser. Today, however, he is recognized not only for the numerous roles he has played in TV shows, in movies, and on the stage, but also as himself. His many public appearances as well as his warmth, charm, charity, modesty, and self-deprecating sense of humor have helped increase his popularity and cement his place as one of today's most popular and respected entertainers.

As Your Host

Harris frequently makes appearances as himself, including several hosting gigs. He served as guest host of the long-running *Saturday Night Live* on NBC in January 2009. During the show, Harris parodied himself in the role as Mark Cohen from *Rent*. He next hosted the *Writers Guild of America Awards* in February 2009 and the *TV Land Awards* that April. He went on to earn a reputation as a truly engaging host on the *63rd Annual Tony Awards* on CBS in June 2009. The show got its highest rating in years, and Harris was praised for his performance as host. Andrew Gans of *Playbill* wrote, "Harris was charming from the moment he stepped onstage," adding that Harris "hosted with an appealing ease."[64] Harris got a laugh from the audience right off the bat when he explained that the opening number that

Harris has made several popular appearances hosting talk shows and awards programs, including the Tony Awards in 2009 and 2011.

night was the most expensive in the history of the Tony Awards, then added, "And that is why *I'm* your host tonight."[65] Despite his self-effacing joke, Harris went on to win an Emmy Award for Outstanding Special Class Program for his job hosting the Tony Awards.

Harris's compelling turn as host of the Tony Awards led to an invitation to host the *61st Primetime Emmy Awards*, also on CBS, that September. In addition to hosting, Harris was also the coproducer of the show. He was also nominated for a best supporting actor award for his role as Barney Stinson on *How I Met Your Mother* (he lost the award to Jon Cryer for his role on *Two and a Half Men*). Reviewer Frank Scheck noted that Harris "did a standout job" and was "affable, charming and simultaneously self-deprecating and comically self-aggrandizing."[66]

More hosting performances followed, including the *Spike Video Game Awards* in December 2010, at which he also won the award for Best Performance by a Human Male for his voice-over work on the video game *Spider-Man: Shattered Dimensions*. In June 2011 Harris returned as host of the *65th Annual Tony Awards* on CBS, again showing his self-mocking sense of humor as he told actress Brooke Shields, "You're so hot you made me think I was straight for twenty-three years."[67]

Harris has made numerous other TV appearances as himself, including a guest appearance on *Sesame Street* in 2008, during which he performed a musical number as the Sesame Street Fairy Shoe Person in a costume that included an off-white suit with wide lapels and feathery wings. He has also appeared in several TV commercials, including one for Comcast in which he has a dual role and two for Old Spice in which he spoofs his role as Doogie Howser.

He has filled in several times for Regis Philbin on *Live with Regis and Kelly* and has been very popular as a guest cohost of the show. Part of his appeal to audiences as a host can be seen in his approach to his hosting duties, in which he carefully considers his viewing audience. As Harris explains, when he serves as guest cohost on *Live with Regis and Kelly*, "I'm not thinking Neil the Actor, I'm thinking, *Housewife, ironing clothes, eleven o'clock.* What kind of thing does she want to see?"[68]

Harris was also a big hit in 2010 when he appeared as one of the guest judges on season nine of the long-running Fox reality TV show *American Idol*. He served as a judge during a round of initial auditions held in Dallas, Texas. He frequently disagreed with and stood up to the notoriously harsh judge Simon Cowell, at one point even exclaiming in frustration that Cowell was not allowing him to speak. A writer for MSNBC said that Harris was "the best of the guest judges to grace the 'Idol' stage so far this season,"[69] and applauded him for standing up to Cowell.

A Love of Magic

Harris's love of magic has led to even more appearances as himself. He is a huge fan of magic and declares, "Magic is my main hobby."[70] In fact, his dressing room on the set of *How I Met Your Mother* is decorated with posters of master magicians, and a bronze skull sits on the coffee table. He has been an amateur magician since he was a teenager and has performed magic tricks on numerous TV shows, including *How I Met Your Mother*, *Glee*, and the *Ellen DeGeneres Show*, in which he asked a very nervous DeGeneres to lie down on a bed of spikes. A teenaged Harris even got the better of *Tonight Show* host Johnny Carson, himself an aficionado of magic, during a 1990 appearance on Carson's show. Harris also likes to perform card tricks and magic tricks for reporters who interview him. For example, during an interview for *People* magazine, he turned a piece of paper into a twenty-dollar bill.

In addition to performing card and magic tricks on TV, Harris serves on the board of directors for the famed Magic Castle. This Los Angeles nightclub built to resemble a castle is for magicians and magic enthusiasts and also serves as the clubhouse for the Academy of Magical Arts. Additionally, Harris hosted the 2008 World Magic Awards in Las Vegas. In 2009 he was the celebrity guest of honor on the reality competition show *Top Chef Masters*, which took place at the Magic Castle. In the episode featuring Harris, contestants were challenged to create the most delectable meal for him.

Harris appears outside of the Magic Castle, home to the Academy of Magical Arts.

The Real Neil

Along with magic, Harris enjoys anything that requires great creativity, skill, and practice. He enjoys activities like treasure hunts and competitive reality games and is a big fan of the reality TV series *Big Brother*. He also likes any type of puzzle and has a collection of especially challenging ones. Slapstick comedy and acrobatics are especially favorite activities of his, and he likes jumping on the trampoline and swinging on the trapeze. Visiting the circus is another favorite pastime, especially the Cirque du Soleil, a Canada-based company whose lavish, theatrical shows dazzle audiences around the world.

Christmas in August

Neil Patrick Harris, a big fan of reality TV, made a surprise visit to the set of the CBS reality show *Big Brother: All Stars* in August 2006. Contestants of this show live and compete together in a large house equipped with cameras and microphones for a chance to win five hundred thousand dollars. Harris arrived on the set wearing a red Santa Claus hat to distribute presents for the Christmas in August reward one of the contestants won. When he entered the house, Harris, who is a huge fan of the show, was in awe at being inside the *Big Brother* house. He woke up the

Harris made a surprise appearance on the CBS reality television show Big Brother *in 2006.*

still sleeping contestants and handed them their presents, which consisted mostly of clothing. Contestant Will Kirby, who is a fan of *How I Met Your Mother*, was ecstatic to meet Neil Patrick Harris in person.

For Harris's thirtieth birthday, his friends created an elaborate surprise party that involved a scavenger hunt, complete with a kidnapping and a horseback ride. Despite his compass, Harris wound up hundreds of feet off course. Knowing Harris would be delighted, David Burtka surprised him on his thirty-eighth birthday in 2011 with another memorable celebration. Harris wrote on his Twitter page: "My b'day was unreal. D created a surprise 'murder mystery' with 25 close friends in character. I was the detective and had to solve crimes! . . . Then, in the backyard, he hired a group of acrobats to do this epic Cirque-like show in/around the pool. With fire!!"[71]

Harris, the lover of anything that has to do with solving riddles or puzzles, was thrilled to discover the reality action-adventure game *Accomplice*. This interactive theatrical experience was conceived by film editor Tom Salamon and his sister Betsy Sufott. Part scavenger hunt and part street theater, the game features a team of participants who follow a set of clues that lead them around the city to various sites. They are guided by actors and must work to untangle some sort of mystery, riddle, or fictitious crime.

Accomplice began in New York City in 2005 and soon headed to London as well. When Harris and some friends took part in a three-hour-long *Accomplice* game in New York, they were hooked. Says Harris, "We were just giddy with the fact that someone had spent the time to create this experience for us."[72] With Harris's help, Salamon brought the game to Hollywood in 2009. In order to maintain the mystery surrounding the game, not many details are given to participants in advance, and Harris, Salamon, and Sufott are careful not to reveal too much when discussing the game.

Neil Lends a Hand

Another way in which Harris expresses himself is through his charity work. He has been involved in activism and charity since he was in his teens. In 1992, for example, he lent his voice to an episode of *Captain Planet and the Planeteers*. This was an animated environmentalist program aimed at kids that aired on TBS from 1990 to 1992. Harris played a high school football player named Todd Andrews who has AIDS and has to face the rumors being spread about him and the disease by his classmates. This episode, titled "A Formula for Hate," was one of the first animated TV shows to deal with the issue of AIDS.

Harris has continued his activism and philanthropic efforts as an adult. After his longtime manager, Booh Schut, developed breast cancer, Harris began fund-raising for cancer research. In particular, he has contributed to Susan G. Komen for the Cure, a foundation that provides care and education for breast cancer sufferers and funds research on cancer prevention and treatment. The charity was founded in 1982 by Nancy G. Brinker after the death of her sister, Susan G. Komen, from breast cancer.

Harris appeared on Celebrity Jeopardy! *in 2010, raising money for Food on Foot, a Los Angeles-based charity and one of many causes that he supports.*

The Earth Day Special

Neil Patrick Harris has long been involved in environmental activism. In 1990 Harris participated in the Time Warner–sponsored *Earth Day Special*. This two-hour special aired on ABC on Earth Day, which is observed each year on April 22. It dealt with environmental issues such as pollution, deforestation, and global warming. Harris appeared as part of an all-star cast that included Queen Latifah, Dan Aykroyd, Meryl Streep, Betty White, Robin Williams, Geena Davis, Morgan Freeman, and Kevin Costner, among many others. The special consisted of a series of skits that were threaded together to help show kids the problems faced by our planet and what can be done to help save the planet. In one skit Bette Midler played Mother Earth, who becomes ill, falls from the sky, and is rushed to the hospital. There, she receives treatment from Harris, in character as Doogie Howser. Harris also stood at a podium as several kids came forward and explained what efforts they were making to help, such as carpooling and recycling. The special also included a skit featuring the Muppets in an ecologically devastated swamp talking about how humans were harming the planet and causing the extinction of wildlife.

Harris has also contributed support to numerous other charities. These include the AIDS Healthcare Foundation, which provides medical aid and advocacy services to AIDS victims regardless of ability to pay; Clothes Off Our Back, which auctions off celebrity outfits with the proceeds benefiting various children's charities; Children International, which offers people the opportunity to sponsor children affected by poverty in eleven countries around the world; Feeding America, which provides meals for people affected by poverty and hunger in the United States; First Book, which provides children from low-income families in North America with access to new, high-quality books; and Hope North, a 40-acre (16.2ha) area in northern Uganda that provides homes, education, and vocational training for refugees, orphans, and former child soldiers.

In May 2010 Harris appeared on an episode of *Celebrity Jeopardy* alongside Cheech Marin and Jane Kaczmarek. The charity Harris played for was Food on Foot, which provides food, clothing, shelter, and job opportunities to homeless, disabled, elderly, and low-income persons in the Los Angeles area. Although Harris lost the game to Cheech Marin, he and Kaczmarek each won one hundred thousand dollars for their respective charities.

An Influential Tweeter

Neil Patrick Harris is perhaps most "himself" on his Twitter account. He is a prolific writer who posts messages about his personal and professional life, sometimes several times a day. His icon is a picture of himself in costume as Dr. Horrible. Harris's posts are often witty and entertaining. For example, on December 31, 2010, he wrote: "Neil's New Year Resolutions, Part 5: Learn to speak baby."[73] At times his posts are much more serious. For example, after attending a Broadway performance of *The Normal Heart*, which depicts the beginnings of the AIDS/HIV crisis, Harris wrote: "Saw The Normal Heart tonight. Riveting. I'm a mess. All gay people should be required to see it. All straight people will be changed by it."[74] His influence via Twitter has been widespread, and *Time* magazine named him to its list of the top 140 most influential tweeters in 2011. As of July 2011 he had nearly 1.6 million followers on Twitter.

However, Harris has shown that he is not above the temptation to post comments online before thoroughly thinking things through. The actor Eric Braeden, who appears on the CBS daytime drama *The Young and the Restless*, had guest starred on *How I Met Your Mother* in 2008 playing Robin's father. In December 2010 he backed out of a repeat guest appearance. Upset by his cancelation, Harris called Braeden a swear word and posted the following comment: "The actor, (Robin's dad) agreed to a cameo, then last night bailed, saying the part wasn't 'substantial' enough."[75] The sixty-nine-year-old Braeden responded that he was disturbed by Harris's choice of words and added that he was still recovering from a recent hip surgery. "I was not about to appear on a show for two lines,"[76] explained Braeden.

Harris regretted his initial Twitter post once he learned the real reason Braeden had canceled his guest appearance. He went back online and posted the following message on his Twitter page: "Now I feel bad for [my] comment. Don't know the guy personally. I'm just fiercely protective of our show."[77] He later made light of the whole situation by posting another New Year's resolution on Twitter: "Try not to insult aged soap stars, especially when you're on the same network."[78]

A Bright Future

The future looks bright indeed for Neil Patrick Harris. In 2011 *How I Met Your Mother* was renewed for two more seasons. Harris has also branched out into directing, something he has been interested in since he and his buddies shot horror spoofs in Albuquerque as teens. "Directing is where I am headed," he predicted in a 1996 interview. "It's my first love."[79]

Harris directed a stage production of the rock musical *Rent*, which played three performances at the Hollywood Bowl in August 2010. Though this was the first time he directed a large-scale stage musical, the fact that he had previously performed in the play helped his debut go smoothly. As Vanessa Hudgens, who appeared in the production at the Hollywood Bowl, put it, "Neil is a real actor's director. He has a lot of experience with the show and so he's clear in what he wants."[80]

In addition to directing a production of *Rent*, Harris also directed the one-hundredth episode of *How I Met Your Mother*, titled "Jenkins," in 2010. In 2011 he directed an as-yet untitled and unreleased TV project that involves an ensemble cast, including Michelle Trachtenberg and Michael Landes.

Already impressively versatile as an actor, Harris has expanded his activities to include directing both stage and television productions.

Whether he chooses to spend his time in front of or behind the camera, one thing is certain—the popularity of former child star Neil Patrick Harris has soared in recent years. His enormous appeal as an entertainer is reflected in the fact that he received a star on the Hollywood Walk of Fame. As Emily Nussbaum of *New York* magazine commented, with his easygoing, affable nature and his many talents, "Harris seems poised to become the first out gay actor to become an A-list star."[81]

Introduction: A Renaissance Man

1. Quoted in Michael A. Lipton. "Postdoctoral." *People,* December 7, 1998, p. 66.
2. Quoted in Larry Smith and Rachel Fershleiser. *It All Changed in an Instant: More Six-Word Memoirs by Writers Famous & Obscure.* New York: Harper Perennial, 2010, p. 181.
3. Emily Nussbaum. "High-Wire Act." New York, September 13, 2009. http://nymag.com/arts/tv/profiles/59002.

Chapter 1: A Young Actor

4. History.com. "Neil Patrick Harris on New Mexico." Video, March 1, 2010. www.history.com/videos/neil-patrick-harris-on-new-mexico.
5. Quoted in Joanne Kaufman. "Neil Patrick Harris Finds a Winning Rx in Doogie Howser." *People,* March 19, 1990, p. 71.
6. Quoted in Kaufman. "Neil Patrick Harris Finds a Winning Rx in Doogie Howser," p. 72.
7. Quoted in Kaufman. "Neil Patrick Harris Finds a Winning Rx in Doogie Howser," p. 72.
8. Quoted in Kaufman. "Neil Patrick Harris Finds a Winning Rx in Doogie Howser," p. 71.
9. Quoted in Kaitlin McCarthy. "Neil Patrick Harris Helps Local Theatre." KRQE.com, August 22, 2010. www.krqe.com/dpp/news/business/neil-patrick-harris-in-nm-for-fundraiser.
10. Quoted in Jan Breslauer. "The Post Whiz-Kid Phase." Los Angeles Times, August 31, 1997. http://articles.latimes.com/1997/aug/31/entertainment/ca-27434.
11. Quoted in Oldsmobile Celebrity Circle. "Neil Patrick Harris Chats on AOL." Transcript, America Online, July 18, 1996. http://chloe74.tripod.com/articles/article5.html.
12. *Variety.* "Clara's Heart." December 31, 1987. www.variety.com/review/VE1117789941?refcatid=31&printerfriendly=true.

13. John J. O'Connor. "'Home Fires Burning': Integrity Amid Substance." New York Times, January 29, 1989. www.nytimes.com/1989/01/29/arts/tv-view-home-fires-burning-integrity-amid-substance.html.

Chapter 2: Becoming a Teenage Star

14. Quoted in Josef Adalian. "The Vulture Transcript: Prolific TV Creator David E. Kelley on His Career Hits and Misses." New York, March 21, 2011. http://nymag.com/daily/entertainment/2011/03/david_e_kelley_interview_wonde.html.
15. Quoted in Kaufman. "Neil Patrick Harris Finds a Winning Rx in Doogie Howser," p. 72.
16. Quoted in Kaufman. "Neil Patrick Harris Finds a Winning Rx in Doogie Howser," p. 72.
17. Quoted in Adalian. "The Vulture Transcript."
18. Quoted in Kaufman. "Neil Patrick Harris Finds a Winning Rx in Doogie Howser," p. 71.
19. Quoted in Nussbaum. "High-Wire Act."
20. Quoted in Kaufman. "Neil Patrick Harris Finds a Winning Rx in Doogie Howser," p. 72.
21. Quoted in Lipton. "Postdoctoral," p. 66.
22. Quoted in Lipton. "Postdoctoral," p. 66.
23. Quoted in Susan King. "Profile: Miles from Doogie." Los Angeles Times, November 21, 1993. http://articles.latimes.com/1993-11-21/news/tv-59138_1_doogie-howser.
24. Quoted in Lipton. "Postdoctoral," p. 66.

Chapter 3: A Challenging Transition

25. Quoted in Michael McGough. "Looking for a Creative Life After 'Doogie Howser M.D.'" New York Times, November 2, 1997. http://chloe74.tripod.com/articles/article11.html.
26. Kenneth Turan. "Stop Buggin' Me!; Based on the Heinlein Novel, 'Starship Troopers Is Directed by Paul Verhoeven with Lots of Attention to Mayhem, Gore, and Goo." Los Angeles Times, November 1, 1997, p. F1.
27. David Nusair. "The Starship Troopers Series." Reel Film Reviews, August 2, 2008. www.reelfilm.com/starship.htm#1.

28. Charles Tatum. "The Proposition (1998)." eFilmCritic.com, March 29, 2003. www.efilmcritic.com/review.php?movie=133.

29. James Berardinelli. "Undercover Brother." Reelviews, 2002. www.reelviews.net/movies/u/undercover_brother.html.

30. Quoted in Nussbaum. "High-Wire Act."

31. Brian McKay. "Harold and Kumar Go to White Castle." eFilm Critic.com, August 1, 2004. www.efilmcritic.com/review. php?movie=9598&reviewer=258&highlight=harold+and+ kumar.

32. Steve Rose. "Harold & Kumar Escape from Guantanamo Bay." Guardian (UK), March 10, 2008. www.guard ian.co.uk/ culture/2008/mar/10/southbysouthwest. festivals3.

33. Neil Patrick Harris. Interview by Julie Chen. *The Early Show*. CBS, October 9, 2006.

34. Quoted in Bill Keveney. "Host Neil Patrick Harris Gives Emmys a Bit of Awesomeness." USA Today, September 14, 2009. www.usatoday.com/life/television/news/2009-09-13-neil-patrick-harris_N.htm.

35. Harris. Interview by Julie Chen.

Chapter 4: Onstage and Behind the Mic

36. Quoted in Oldsmobile Celebrity Circle. "Neil Patrick Harris Chats on AOL."

37. Linda Winer. "'Luck': Is There a Doctor in the House?" *Newsday,* April 5, 1995.

38. Quoted in Lipton. "Postdoctoral," p. 67.

39. Quoted in McGough. "Looking for a Creative Life After 'Doogie Howser M.D.'"

40. Quoted in Lipton. "Postdoctoral," p. 67.

41. Quoted in Breslauer. "The Post Whiz-Kid Phase."

42. Peter Marks. "Theater Review: Such Rib-Sticking Meat Pies!" New York Times, March 18, 1999. http://theater.nytimes. com/mem/theater/treview.html?res=9B05E7DF1631F93BA 25750C0A96F958260&scp=1&sq=Sweeny%20Todd%20r eview%20neil%20patrick%20harris&st=cse.

43. Bruce Weber. "Theater Review: Light, Quick Anne Heche Makes 'Proof' a New Play." New York Times, July 19, 2002.

www.nytimes.com/2002/07/19/movies/theater-review-a-light-quick-anne-heche-makes-proof-a-new-play.html?scp=1&sq=review%20proof%20neil%20patrick%20harris&st=cse.

44. *New York Times*. "Sondheim with a Twist." May 11, 2004. http://community.nytimes.com/rate-review/theater.nytimes.com/show/7044/Assassins/overview?scp=3&sq=assassins%20review%20neil%20patrick%20harris&st=cse.

45. Neil Patrick Harris. 1st Annual Streamy Awards acceptance speech, March 28, 2009. http://watch.streamys.org/go/?p=13.

46. Quoted in People.com. "Neil Patrick Harris Uses His Spider Sense." Video, September 14, 2010. www.people.com/people/article/0,,20009134,00.html.

47. Quoted in Oldsmobile Celebrity Circle. "Neil Patrick Harris Chats on AOL."

Chapter 5: Shattering the Glass Closet

48. Quoted in *People*. "Neil Patrick Harris: 'I Am a Very Content Gay Man.'" November 20, 2006, p. 81.

49. Nussbaum. "High-Wire Act."

50. Quoted in Michel Martin. "When Gay News (or Crisis) Hits Hollywood, Gay Public Relations Guru Shines." Transcript, NPR, March 8, 2010. www.npr.org/templates/story/story.php?storyId=124459333.

51. Nussbaum. "High-Wire Act."

52. Quoted in People. "Neil Patrick Harris," p. 81.

53. Jed Dreben and Tim Nudd. "Neil Patrick Harris Weighs In on Grey's Spat." People, January 19, 2007. www.people.com/people/article/0,,20009134,00.html.

54. Quoted in Martin. "When Gay News (or Crisis) Hits Hollywood, Gay Public Relations Guru Shines."

55. Quoted in Julie Jordan. "Neil Patrick Harris & David Burtka: Thrilled to Be Raising Twins." People, December 29, 2010. www.people.com/people/article/0,,20453492,00.html.

56. Neil Patrick Harris. Twitter, October 15, 2010. http://twitter.com/#!/ActuallyNPH.

57. David Burtka. Twitter, June 24, 2011. http://twitter.com/#!/Davidburtka.

58. Neil Patrick Harris. Twitter, June 26, 2011. http://twitter.com/#!/ActuallyNPH.

59. Neil Patrick Harris. Twitter, June 24, 2011. http://twitter.com/#!/ActuallyNPH.

60. Neil Patrick Harris. Twitter, December 9, 2010. http://twitter.com/#!/ActuallyNPH.

61. Neil Patrick Harris. Twitter, December 18, 2010. http://twitter.com/#!/ActuallyNPH.

62. Neil Patrick Harris. "Neil Patrick Harris Knows That Hurting Yourself Is Not the Answer." MTV News, October 4, 2010. www.mtv.com/videos/news/579191/neil-patrick-harris-knows-that-hurting-yourself-is-not-the-answer.jhtml.

63. Quoted in Keveney. "Host Neil Patrick Harris Gives Emmys a Bit of Awesomeness."

Chapter 6: Neil Patrick Harris as Neil Patrick Harris

64. Andrew Gans. "Diva Talk: 2009 Tony Awards Recap Plus News of Block, Graff and Hilty." Playbill, June 12, 2009. www.playbill.com/celebritybuzz/article/130202-DIVA-TALK-2009-Tony-Awards-Recap-Plus-News-of-Block-Graff-and-Hilty/pg2.

65. Neil Patrick Harris. *63rd Annual Tony Awards*. CBS, June 7, 2009.

66. Frank Scheck. "Emmy Awards Get Boost from Neil Patrick Harris." Reuters, September 21, 2009. www.reuters.com/article/2009/09/21/us-television-emmys-review-idUSTRE58K0MA20090921.

67. Neil Patrick Harris. *65th Annual Tony Awards*. CBS, June 12, 2011.

68. Quoted in Nussbaum. "High-Wire Act."

69. Craig Berman. "Neil Patrick Harris Shines in Dallas for 'Idol.'" MSNBC.com, January 27, 2010. http://today.msnbc.msn.com/id/35111583/ns/today-entertainment/t/neil-patrick-harris-shines-dallas-idol.

70. Quoted in Oldsmobile Celebrity Circle. "Neil Patrick Harris Chats on AOL."

71. Neil Patrick Harris. Twitter, June 16, 2011. http://twitter.com/#!/ActuallyNPH.

72. Quoted in Los Angeles Times. "'Accomplice' Goes Hollywood." April 26, 2009. http://latimesblogs.latimes.com/culturemonster/2009/04/accomplice-goes-hollywood.html.

73. Neil Patrick Harris. Twitter, December 31, 2010. http://twitter.com/#!/ActuallyNPH.

74. Neil Patrick Harris. Twitter, June 3, 2011. http://twitter.com/#!/ActuallyNPH.

75. Neil Patrick Harris. Twitter, December 17, 2010. http://twitter.com/#!/ActuallyNPH.

76. Quoted in Alla Byrne. "Neil Patrick Harris Regrets Bashing Actor on Twitter." People, December 18, 2010. www.people.com/people/article/0,20452019,00.html.

77. Neil Patrick Harris. Twitter, December 17, 2010. http://twitter.com/#!/ActuallyNPH.

78. Neil Patrick Harris. Twitter, December 31, 2010. http://twitter.com/#!/ActuallyNPH.

79. Quoted in Oldsmobile Celebrity Circle. "Neil Patrick Harris Chats on AOL."

80. Quoted in David Ng. "Neil Patrick Harris' New "Rent" Role: Director." Los Angeles Times, August 4, 2010. http://articles.latimes.com/2010/aug/04/entertainment/la-et-neil-patrick-harris-rent-20100804.

81. Nussbaum. "High-Wire Act."

1973

Neil Patrick Harris is born on June 15 in Albuquerque, New Mexico.

1979

Wins the part of Toto in a school production of *The Wizard of Oz*; begins appearing onstage every chance he gets.

1987

Discovered at drama camp in Las Cruces, New Mexico, by playwright Mark Medoff.

1988

Clara's Heart, his debut film, is released; also appears in the children's classic *Purple People Eater* and the TV movie *Too Good to Be True.*

1989

Nominated for a Young Artist Award and a Golden Globe for *Clara's Heart*; appears in the TV movies *Cold Sassy Tree* and *Home Fires Burning*; is tapped by Steven Bochco to play the lead role in *Doogie Howser, M.D.*

1991

Appears in the made-for-TV movie *Stranger in the Family*; graduates with honors from La Cueva High School; provides voice-over work for an episode of *The Simpsons.*

1992

Wins a Young Artist Award for Best Young Actor Starring in a Television Series for the third year in a row; begins voicing a young mouse named Max in the animated ABC series *Capitol Critters.*

1993

Guest stars on the NBC science-fiction series *Quantum Leap* and the CBS mystery series *Murder She Wrote*; ABC abruptly cancels *Doogie Howser*.

1994

Makes his New York stage debut in the play *Luck, Pluck & Virtue*.

1997

Costars in the science-fiction film *Starship Troopers*; makes his musical stage debut as aspiring filmmaker Mark Cohen in the play *Rent*.

1998

Appears in the film *The Proposition*; plays Romeo onstage in a production of *Romeo and Juliet* at San Diego's Old Globe Theatre.

1999

Costars in the short-lived NBC sitcom *Stark Raving Mad*; plays Tobias Ragg in Los Angeles concert performance of Stephen Sondheim's *Sweeney Todd*.

2000

Reprises his role as Tobias Ragg in *Sweeney Todd* at Lincoln Center in New York; the performance is released as a CD called *Sweeney Todd: Live in Concert*.

2001

Appears as Ragg again in San Francisco with the San Francisco Symphony; the production is taped and broadcast on PBS and later released on DVD.

2002

Makes his Broadway debut in the drama *Proof*.

2003

Appears on Broadway again in as the Emcee in a revival of the musical *Cabaret*; meets fellow actor David Burtka while both are appearing on Broadway.

2004

Plays a highly fictionalized version of himself in the movie *Harold & Kumar Go to White Castle*; appears onstage in Culver City, California, in the play *The Paris Letter*; performs in a Broadway revival of the Sondheim musical *Assassins*; begins dating Burtka.

2005

Cast as lovable cad Barney Stinson in the CBS sitcom *How I Met Your Mother*.

2006

Harris announces publicly that he is gay.

2007

Nominated for an Emmy Award for Outstanding Supporting Actor in a Comedy Series for his role on *How I Met Your Mother*.

2008

Reprises his role as "Neil Patrick Harris" in *Harold & Kumar Escape from Guantanamo Bay*; appears as the title character in the campy Internet musical *Dr. Horrible's Sing-Along Blog*; hosts the World Magic Awards in Las Vegas.

2009

Guest hosts NBC's *Saturday Night Live*; hosts the *63rd Annual Tony Awards* and the *61st Primetime Emmy Awards*; provides the voice for Steve, the Flint family's pet monkey, in the computer-animated film *Cloudy with a Chance of Meatballs*.

2010

Guest stars on the Fox comedy-drama *Glee* and sings the Aerosmith classic song "Dream On," an appearance that wins him the Emmy Award for Outstanding Guest Performance by a Male Actor in a Comedy Series; directs a stage production of the rock musical *Rent* at the Hollywood Bowl; Harris and Burtka welcome twins Gideon Scott and Harper Grace.

2011

Receives a star on the Hollywood Walk of Fame; hosts the *65th Annual Tony Awards*; via Twitter, announces his plans to marry Burtka.

Books

John Grogan. *A Very Marley Christmas*. New York: HarperChildren's Audio, 2008. Harris lends his voice to this children's audiobook about the lovable puppy who wreaks havoc for his family over the holidays.

Elmore Leonard. *A Coyote's in the House*. New York: HarperChildren's Audio, 2004. Harris narrates this children's audiobook about a talking coyote who goes to Hollywood.

Joseph Olshan. *Clara's Heart*. London: Bloomsbury UK, 1998. This novel is the basis for the film of the same name in which Harris made his debut as a young boy torn apart by his parents' marital troubles.

Jim Steinmeyer. *Hiding the Elephant: How Magicians Invented the Impossible and Learned to Disappear*. New York: Carrol & Graf, 2004. A theatrical special effects expert presents a history of stage magic and explanations of how magicians perform various illusions, including Harry Houdini's famous disappearing elephant. The foreword was written by Teller of Penn & Teller.

Larry Stempel. *Showtime: A History of the Broadway Musical Theater*. New York: Norton, 2010. This book examines musicals both on and off Broadway and offers a look at their history from the mid-nineteenth century to the present day. Includes sections on *Rent* and *Cabaret*.

Barney Stinson with Matt Kuhn. *Bro on the Go*. New York: Fireside, 2009. A satirical reference guide offering rules and inspiration for men written by Neil Patrick Harris's *How I Met Your Mother* character Barney Stinson.

Periodicals

Jan Breslauer. "The Post Whiz-Kid Phase." *Los Angeles Times*, August 31, 1997.

Jeannette Catsoulis. "Posing as a Poet for the Sake of a Child's Education." Review, *New York Times*, June 23, 2011.

Jed Dreben and Tim Nudd. "Neil Patrick Harris Weighs In on *Grey's* Spat." *People*, January 19, 2007.

Peter Hartlaub. "Neil Patrick Harris Up for Sketchfest Challenge." *San Francisco Chronicle*, January 12, 2010.

Greg Hernandez. "Neil Patrick Harris Chats with Entertainment Weekly About Hosting Sunday's Emmy Awards." *Entertainment Weekly*, September 19, 2009.

Julie Jordan. "Neil Patrick Harris & David Burtka: Thrilled to Be Raising Twins." *People*, December 29, 2010.

Joanne Kaufman. "Neil Patrick Harris Finds a Winning Rx in Doogie Howser." *People*, March 19, 1990.

People. "Neil Patrick Harris: 'I Am a Very Content Gay Man.'" November 20, 2006.

Internet Sources

Craig Berman. "Neil Patrick Harris Shines in Dallas for 'Idol.'" MSNBC.com, January 27, 2010. http://today.msnbc.msn.com/id/35111583/ns/today-entertainment/t/neil-patrick-harris-shines-dallas-idol.

Alla Byrne. "Neil Patrick Harris Regrets Bashing Actor on Twitter." *People*, December 18, 2010. www.people.com/people/article/0,20452019,00.html.

Detroit Free Press. "Neil Patrick Harris Ready to Wed After Vote." June 27, 2011. www.freep.com/article/20110627/ENT07/106270361/Neil-Patrick-Harris-ready-wed-after-vote.

Bill Keveney. "Host Neil Patrick Harris Gives Emmys a Bit of Awesomeness." *USA Today*, September 14, 2009. www.usatoday.com/life/television/news/2009-09-13-neil-patrick-harris_N.htm.

Michel Martin. "When Gay News (or Crisis) Hits Hollywood, Gay Public Relations Guru Shines." Transcript, NPR, March 8, 2010. www.npr.org/templates/story/story.php?storyId=124459333.

Kaitlin McCarthy. "Neil Patrick Harris Helps Local Theatre." KRQE.com, August 22, 2010. www.krqe.com/dpp/news/business/neil-patrick-harris-in-nm-for-fundraiser.

Emily Nussbaum. "High-Wire Act." *New York*, September 13, 2009. http://nymag.com/arts/tv/profiles/59002.

Oldsmobile Celebrity Circle. "Neil Patrick Harris Chats on AOL." Transcript, America Online, July 18, 1996. http://chloe74.tripod.com/articles/article5.html.

Ileane Rudolph. "Neil Patrick Harris Suits Up to Host the Tony Awards." *TV Guide*, June 10, 2011. www.tvguide.com/News/Neil-Patrick-Harris-1034084.aspx.

Frank Scheck. "Emmy Awards Get Boost from Neil Patrick Harris." Reuters, September 21, 2009. www.reuters.com/article/2009/09/21/us-television-emmys-review-idUSTRE58K0MA20090921.

Michael Schneider. "Oprah, Neil Patrick Harris, Tina Fey to Get Hollywood Walk of Fame Stars." *Variety*, June 17, 2010. http://weblogs.variety.com/on_the_air/2010/06/oprah-neil-patrick-harris-tina-fey-to-get-hollywood-walk-of-fame-stars.html.

Websites

Doogie Howser, M.D. (www.fanpop.com/spots/doogie-howser-md). This fan site is dedicated to the TV show that helped launch Neil Patrick Harris's career. It includes videos, articles, a Doogie quiz, a forum, and much more.

How I Met Your Mother (www.cbs.com/primetime/how_i_met_your_mother). This is the official CBS Entertainment website for the hit TV show costarring Neil Patrick Harris. The site includes photos, video clips and full episodes, information about the cast, a forum, and much more.

Neil Patrick Harris Fan, *CBS Watch Magazine* (http://nph-fan.com). This fan site hosted by *CBS Watch Magazine* includes news, information about upcoming events, photos, videos, tweets, and links to current projects featuring Harris.

Neil Patrick Harris on Twitter (http://twitter.com/#!/ ActuallyNPH). This is Harris's Twitter page, where he writes daily his about his thoughts and insights as well as events pertaining to his career.

Neil Patrick Harris, *People* (www.people.com/people/neil_ patrick_harris). This site contains a wealth of information on Harris, including links to news articles, TV listings, photos, and a biography.

Cherese Cartlidge holds a bachelor's degree in psychology and a master's degree in education. She currently works as a writer and editor and is the author of numerous books for children and young adults, including biographies of Drew Barrymore, Leonardo DiCaprio, Jennifer Hudson, and Taylor Swift. Cartlidge lives in Georgia with her two children.